# DEVELOPMENTAL ACTIVITIES FOR CHILDREN IN SPECIAL EDUCATION

# Developmental
# Activities
# for Children
# in Special Education

*By*

**CYNTHA C. HIRST, M.S.P.E.**

*Assistant Professor*

*and*

**ELAINE MICHAELIS, M.S.**

*Assistant Professor*

*Department of Physical Education*
*Brigham Young University*
*Provo, Utah*

**CHARLES C THOMAS · PUBLISHER**

*Springfield · Illinois · U.S.A.*

*Published and Distributed Throughout the World by*

CHARLES C THOMAS • PUBLISHER

BANNERSTONE HOUSE

301-327 East Lawrence Avenue, Springfield, Illinois, U.S.A.

© *1972, by* CHARLES C THOMAS • PUBLISHER

ISBN 0-398-02313-1

Library of Congress Catalog Card Number: 76-180817

*With* THOMAS BOOKS *careful attention is given to all details of manufacturing and design. It is the Publisher's desire to present books that are satisfactory as to their physical qualities and artistic possibilities and appropriate for their particular use.* THOMAS BOOKS *will be true to those laws of quality that assure a good name and good will.*

*Printed in the United States of America*

*N-1*

# PREFACE

T HE EDUCATION of the more than four million mentally retarded persons in the United States cannot be left only to the "do-gooders" in our society. The United States Government guarantees educational opportunities to all children in the United States through the local public school systems. No longer do parents of mentally retarded children have to pay private school or day care center tuition for the education of their children. These children are part of the public school enrollment, and in some school districts this increased population in the special education program has placed great stress on the numbers of available teachers in this specialized area of education. Teacher training departments in colleges and universities are training teachers with specialization in special education, but the number of students selecting this preparation is far short of the general need in the United States as a whole. Consequently, many teachers who are now in the process of teaching retarded children are not prepared in the fields of special education. They are experienced teachers of elementary education who have been brought into the special education classroom after attending a summer workshop designed to prepare them for the teaching of the retarded.

Physical education is a part of the educational system and is included in the curriculum of most school districts. Preparation of teachers in physical education for the retarded has not yet reached any great degree in the teacher training institutions; however, universities and the Joseph P. Kennedy Foundation have cooperated to start this teacher preparation at the graduate and undergraduate levels, and progress is being made in providing those students who are now involved in their teacher training with the skills necessary to teach physical education activities. The text is being written for those teachers whose training was in the field of special education with no specialization in physical education. The sequences in the text range from the most simple and basic analysis to the complex and complete stunt or skill in a variety of activities. Emphasis has been placed upon skill identification and analysis so that the teacher will have the knowledge and experience necessary to actually teach the retarded child instead of merely keeping him contented and free from frustration for the days of the school year.

This text is also being written to provide an elementary progression of activity presentations for those leaders employed at the many training centers for the handicapped—leaders who are not certified teachers but who have a great deal of responsibility for the education of the retarded and learning-disabled children enrolled in their schools.

The purpose of this book is to present a program of physical activities which will help the child with learning disabilities to develop, according to his own potential, those physical skills necessary for enjoyable living. An attempt has also been made to integrate the development of other academic skills into the practice activities presented for physical development. The authors do not present this material as a prescriptive approach, but rather as a progressive developmental curriculum of activities to aid learning. The development of perceptual as well as motor skills is an anticipated outcome of the program contained in the book. There is no attempt on the part of the authors to suggest for the classroom teacher a curriculum for the teaching of academic concepts. However, an attempt has been made to demonstrate an integrated learning approach which will enhance the learning of academic concepts more efficiently because of the use of additional motivation, learning tools—namely, the kinesthetic sense—and the resultant development of other perceptual senses. Our progressions for each type of activity are presented so the teacher can find a starting place for each child, whether he be a beginner or an experienced performer.

The authors express appreciation to the children who served as models and to their parents who gave permission for the photographs.

C.C.H.

E.M.

# CONTENTS

# DEVELOPMENTAL
# ACTIVITIES
# FOR CHILDREN
# IN SPECIAL EDUCATION

# Chapter 1

# PHYSICAL ACTIVITY IN SPECIAL EDUCATION

Children differ greatly in their ability to adjust to the school situation. Their intellectual ability, habits, attitudes, and expectations vary considerably. The children come from a variety of environments and have had a variety of experiences upon which to rely for future learning.

As the learning experiences are presented in the formal school environment, it becomes apparent that some pupils never seem quite able to learn what others are learning. These difficulties begin early in the school experience and can be noted in the "readiness" experiences which precede formal instruction of subject matter. As the school experience progresses, these children fall further and further behind until they are not able to participate on the same level with rest of the group. The longer they remain in this situation, the more confused they become and the more constantly they are faced with their failure to achieve. Many of their problems may be attributed to a lack of readiness skills. The slow learner in this situation may be lacking merely because of a slow developmental environmental experience, a physical handicap, or an emotional disturbance; or he may be mentally retarded.

The complex environment in which we live demands learning. Learning is difficult enough when all of the influences are good. For a child whose physiological and neurological processes do not operate normally, very special help becomes necessary. Our civilization, while increasing its demands for knowledge, is decreasing the opportunity which it offers for a child to gain the necessary experiences with basic skills. For example, one common problem among children entering school is the lack of basic perceptual-motor skills. Children with this problem will need an opportunity to be taught, to experiment, and to practice activities which build the sensory-motor skills which are required by the more complex activities of reading, writing, and mathematics.

Traditionally, education has approached children by way of the intellectual aspect, mainly through the spoken language. Yet, in the developmental pattern of children, the small muscle skills and the abstract thinking aspects of personality functioning do not make their appearances for quite some time after birth because of the considerable practice necessary for their development. The early life of a child is largely physical in nature. Physical play is his central interest and means of learning. Therefore, activity can and should be a prime method through which learning experiences are provided by the teacher and parent.

Not only is physical activity a valuable teaching aid, but it is also a necessity for good health, without which one loses the desire to be active in play and to achieve. Physical activity keeps the body systems functioning efficiently and provides energy for play activities from which to learn.

*reasons) for P.E.*

## THE VALUE OF ACTIVITY

*Physical Development.* Physical activity contributes toward muscular strength and coordination, endurance, good posture habits, poise, and grace. An interest in one's own potential physical condition, ability, and well-being is stimulated and the ability to appropriately relax may also be learned.

*Emotional Stability.* Play activities provide opportunity for emotional expression and the release of tensions and aggressions. The development of courage, initiative, and alertness result from successful experiences in group and individual games.

*Creativity.* Play provides experiences for creative expression and helps to develop an appreciation of beauty and the aesthetic qualities in life.

*Skill Development.* Opportunity is provided through activity to develop skills basic to future participation in directed learning and leisure time activities. Knowledge of talents and abilities basic for future development may be acquired.

*Social Relationships.* Children learn to exist as members of a group and become cooperative social beings. Through play experiences, the child can learn about the world around him and the laws covering his relationships to the world. In our society, the ability to perform basic motor skills is important to the child and dictates his acceptance and opportunity to participate in the peer activities in the neighborhood. The child needs as many experiences as possible to improve his background, and these experiences should be mostly successful ones.

*Intellectual Development.* From childhood, motor experimentation and learning are the foundations upon which the child learns about himself and the world around him, and they are the premise upon which knowledge is based. It is logical that behavior develops out of muscular activity and that higher forms of behavior are dependent upon lower forms of behavior. There is evidence that the scholastic achievement of mentally retarded children can be improved if supplemented by a proper program of physical education.

*Body Image.* Children form a body image which is based to a great extent upon capabilities gained from bodily movements. This image is basic to the developing personality. Remedial physical developmental work is capable of activating dormant potential for personality development.

## DEVELOPMENTAL SKILLS

It is apparent that readiness to learn regular academic subject matter involves certain basic skills, physical development, and emotional maturity. These skills are the background for the ability and desire to learn concepts of the standard curriculum and for desirable physical performance. These skills are expected of normal children before they reach school age. Since learning is based upon earlier learning, a slow learner may find himself in ever-increasing difficulty without these skills. An opportunity to attain these skills must be provided for the slow learner in order to facilitate a fruitful learning experience.

*Motor Skills.* Basic motor activities involving large portions of the body are involved in tasks such as drawing. This task requires the ability to control the body, to move the fingers, hand, and arm in a coordinated manner, and the ability to differentiate a specific movement pattern out of a general total movement.

*Laterality.* The human body is neurologically and anatomically designed as a bilateral (two-sided) organism. The sides of the body are innervated separately, which makes it possible for unified or separate movements of the respective sides (right or left) of the body. The development of the concept of laterality in movement as it relates to direction in space is a basic fundamental which is necessary to understand one's environment. Laterality is learned through experimentation with body movements and the realization of possible interaction between the two sides of the body and space.

Laterality is not "handedness." It is the awareness of the two sides of the body and their differences. A child will need to develop dominance by developing one side as the leading side. Before learning to write, a child must be able to control both sides of the body separately and simultaneously. The development of laterality is important in distinguishing the difference between objects such as "b" and "d."

*Directionality.* Horizontal, vertical, and depth dimensions follow the understanding of laterality. Kinesthetic awareness is the means by which these concepts are developed. Visual responses are matched with the kinesthetic sense of feeling body parts move to coordinate and evaluate movement. By experimenting with movement patterns, a child learns what movements he must make to touch an object at his right. The coordination of the stimuli from the eyes and the information gained through kinesthetic activity is very important. In order to learn this, a child must make a series of matches between positions of the eyes and positions of the hand in relation to an object. Directionality is dependent upon the development of laterality. Motor activity is the means by which these concepts are learned. It is important that motor learning opportunities be provided and directed toward the development of these skills.

*Posture.* Posture is maintenance of the position of the body with reference to its center of gravity by the innervation of anti-gravity muscle groups. All other movement patterns develop out of basic posture, which is the means by which we relate to our environment. The ability to adjust efficiently body positions to meet purposes of usefulness is important in relating to our environment.

*Body Image.* Our body is the point of reference from which we organize and construct the relative impressions which we receive into a coherent personality. A false conception of one's body image will result in faulty actions and faulty perception of others. The body image is a learned concept which results from the experimentation with body parts and the realization of their relationship to each other and to the external environment. The development of laterality and directionality is an important aspect in the development of a body image.

*Perceptual Discrimination.* The ability to distinguish the visual characteristics of environmental objects and to discriminate the meaning of verbal sounds is important.

*Visual Discrimination.* As a child develops the ability to discriminate the details of the mass before him, he progresses toward a higher form of perception. As he learns to discriminate the details, he also must learn to differentiate details and organize them into form. The ability to differentiate is very important to a child who is trying to analyze forms and learn to read.

*Auditory Discrimination.* To understand language, a person must be receptive to auditory stimulation and be able to discriminate one sound from another. When he is able to do this, he can attach meaning to the sounds and understand combinations of sounds which are appropriate for language. School experiences should provide opportunities to associate language with their activities.

*Spatial Discrimination.* Information about space is gathered through clues which must be interpreted to obtain a concept of space. Kinesthesis is the most direct source of information about space. We compare, select, group, and organize characteristics which become concepts about space.

*Quality Discrimination.* Concepts concerning motion, quality, time, comparison, and location are necessary for learning. A background involving the concepts of fast, slow, when, what, before, after, thicker, up, direct, and so forth is necessary for learning.

*Language Development.* Language usage is developed primarily in the home. Children from culturally deprived areas may be deprived of good language development experiences. It is important that an opportunity to express observations and experiences be provided so the children learn to use these skills. Many games and activities of children are conducive to natural involvement of verbal skills. Singing games, counting scores, using appropriate terminology, and verbalizing exchange of position, accomplishments, or decisions will help to stimulate the use of language.

*Memory.* One of the important variables involved in perceptual process is that of consistent input for similar experimental situations. Since a great number of a child's experiences are motor oriented, it is important that this experience be consistent with the desired learning experiences of the total learning situation. This also affords good opportunity to reinforce learned concepts related to the activity period through integrated learning opportunities.

*Group Association.* Social development and adjustment to the group are important for the slow learner if he is to participate effectively in his environment. Learning to share with the group and to work and play with other individuals is especially necessary. The ability to follow directions, to obey rules and regulations, and to accept decisions and discipline are characteristics which are desirable and which may be developed through group activities.

*Motivation.* Motivation is dependent upon the ability of the teacher to help the child overcome the feeling of inadequacy and to promote success. Coordination of activities to promote understanding and practical application of concepts learned will help to keep the child's interest and to reinforce learning. The activities should be meaningful and should encourage pupil discovery of relationships between the learning situation and his environment. Variety in the teaching approach of activities which require continued practice is necessary for continued interest. Activities should be centered around the abilities and interests of the children.

## PRINCIPLES OF TEACHING

The use of sound teaching techniques is important when teaching any child or any subject. However, because of the nature of the slow learner, good teaching is mandatory. The following suggestions may prove helpful in teaching the slow learner:

1. The children should be ready to learn the specific concept or skill being taught. When a new concept or skill is to be presented, the initial step is to develop a need for it. Next, provide sufficient positive practice or repetitions to make its use accurate and efficient. Numerous situations should then be introduced where the skill is required, thus providing review and application.

2. Instruction should be at the child's level. Verbal directions should be few and very simple, and given without talking down to the child.

3. Instruction should always start with the familiar and proceed to the unfamiliar.

4. The activity should be meaningful and have value to the child. Skills and concepts should be taught through the use of socially meaningful situations and materials. Activities should be presented in terms of the individual's needs and objectives.

5. Plan guaranteed successes. Nothing contributes to interest in an activity more than does legitimate success.

6. Instruction should be planned to encourage transfer of learning. Instruction should be organized and taught systematically to provide for transfer of learning.

7. Repetitions and practice should be used to ensure learning and retention. Practice periods should be short, and new activities should be presented early in the period.

8. Demonstrations and leader participation are good teaching devices. Kinesthetic guidance through correct actions is effective in establishing more efficient patterns of movement.

9. Genuine praise and encouragement are valuable motivators.

10. Class periods should be well organized and supervised.

11. Skills should be presented in a progressive plan by building skill upon skill.

12. Opportunity should be provided for the children to use learned academic skills as they relate to and integrate with the physical activity being presented. (See integration of aquatic skills, Chap. 10.)

13. Class organization should provide for active participation by all, be varied in interests, provide for varied attention span, provide purposeful practice, and create interest in the activity.

14. Safety should be considered in planning the activities.

15. Progress slowly but go as fast as the child is able. When one skill is learned move quickly to the next. Do not get discouraged. Progress is slow with some nonretardates, so be happy about the smallest progress.

16. Develop a close relationship with the child. Show how pleased you are when he is able to do even the most elementary skill correctly. Let him show you many times the skill he has learned. Let him show other adults and other children. Let him know you sincerely want him to perform, and reward him with praise.

17. Be secure in your knowledge of the skills. To participate in this program you do not need to be an expert performer yourself, but you should be able to do the skills you are asking the child to do.

18. Keep the lesson fun. The child will learn faster if he enjoys what is being done. Entertainment is not a primary objective of a physical education program, but enjoyment is a tool which increases learning.

19. Keep the instruction period short. During an instruction period the child can only practice up to his own limits of concentration; these limits may be broadened, but only the child can determine this. Allow his attention to wander only after he has really tried to perform. When his attention does wander, change the skill, show him another game, but return to the desired performance before the instructional period is over.

20. Be patient, but be forceful. Help the child succeed by encouraging him to perform the skill on which you are working.

21. Develop group instruction as soon as possible. The sooner a child can function in a group, the sooner he will be able to live in a group.

22. Demand good discipline. A child will learn more if he is required to be well behaved. He will also learn better how to function with a group when his good behavior is required. Use firmness and fairness, but remember you are dealing with a small child.

23. As far as is possible have the same instructor each day. A child responds better when he feels secure with the instructor. He should not have to adjust every period to another teacher.

24. If you need to touch a child during the lesson, tell him about it before you do so. If he is expecting you to take hold of his hands, he will willingly permit you to. If he is surprised, he may pull back, and you will have to repeat the procedure.

The activities presented in the following chapters have been included and planned to provide desirable learning materials to meet the needs of the special child with learning disabilities and to provide for his total development toward normalcy. When the child is able to participate successfully in these activities, he should be guided into programs with normal children.

# Chapter 2

# MOVEMENT EXPLORATION AND MOTOR-PERCEPTUAL ACTIVITIES

MOST MENTALLY HANDICAPPED CHILDREN are limited in their ability to move. This inability may be the result of a physical handicap or a lack of opportunity to develop physical skills. The lack of opportunity may be the result of the social environment or educational opportunity. Because of insecurity some children with an able physical body may be afraid to walk down the stairs or to walk over a bridge. After experiencing a gradual approach in movement exploration, a child, because of the additional experiences he gets through physical activity, may gain confidence and become more able to perform physical tasks and gain more depth in understanding.

The activities in this chapter are designed to provide not only for good physical development but for an integrated learning experience. These activities provide an opportunity for the student to develop movement skills, body image, and concepts about space, time, direction, dimension, speed, quality, rhythm, and mood.

In the following presentation the basic activity, such as a walk, is presented. The activity is then varied by changing one of the elements of the movement. By changing an element of the movement, the learned pattern provides a basis for new learning involving a new concept. This transfer of learning is difficult for mentally handicapped children, and yet learning, which is based on past experience, must be related to the frame of reference of each child. By designing the movement activities in this manner, a basis for learning the necessary concepts is present. Movement provides an additional sense to aid learning. This sense is kinesthetic awareness. By using the proprioceptors or sense organs in the muscles as an additional feedback for learning, many concepts can be learned easier.

The activities presented in this chapter represent a basic approach for most children. There are many possibilities for development, and the procedure may be varied to meet the needs of the individual child.

The purpose of a unit on movement exploration is to provide as many varied experiences for the child as possible and thus encourage him to explore what his body can do and how to do it best. The experiences should be designed to reinforce previously learned patterns and to build toward new patterns and experiences.

For normal children the usual approach is to present the exploration activity in the form of a problem. The child then proceeds to explore the environment with his body, learning and creating new patterns and understandings. For example, "How many different movements can you do with one arm?" For mentally handicapped children the activity usually will need to be more structured toward the achievement of the desired movement goal. An example might be, "Lift your arm high, move your arm to the side," and so on. These activities should be designed to integrate the learning experience by learning new concepts and increasing the vocabulary while learning about the body and movement patterns. The possibilities for learning are unlimited.

Movement exploration is a good way to stimulate and motivate a child to learn and progress in his development. Everyone can find success, whether it be a slight movement or a vigorous fling of the arm. Recognition should be given to each child for his accomplishment. Encouragement to use his body to its fullest range of movement and to associate verbal expression of learned concepts should be a part of the recognition of success.

This unit includes the basic skills of movement which are the fundamentals of life's movement experiences. These basic skills include eight locomotor skills and six nonlocomotor skills. The ability to perform these skills is basic to successful participation in rhythms, games, and self-testing activities which children enjoy. Experiences which provide the child with an opportunity to learn these basic skills in a nonstressful, successful setting will prepare him for activities more complex in nature.

The movement experiences have been designed to develop progressively from a nonmobile position to various locomotor activities. The activities progress from unilateral to bilateral movements and encourage the development of basic motor skills, good posture, concepts of laterality and directionality, memory, and language usage.

The suggested activities include tasks requiring different levels of involvement. Some are very simple while others require more ability to understand and to do. The teacher should select the appropriate task for the child and adjust the other problems to meet the ability of the child.

## PRINCIPLES OF MOVEMENT

When the basic principles of movement are applied to the skills, the efficiency of the skills can be improved. The three principles explained below are basic enough for all children to apply.

### Principle of Opposition

When a balanced, maximum effort is desired in the movement, the sides of the body work in opposition. For example, in throwing a ball for distance, if you throw with the right arm, you step onto the left foot. This will allow for the total body to contribute to the action and still maintain balance. Walking is another example of opposition in movement—the opposite arm swings forward as each forward step is taken. When accuracy rather than force becomes the main objective of the action, as in throwing darts, opposition is eliminated; therefore fewer body parts are involved in the movement and there is less chance of an error in the performance.

### Principle of Total Body Assembly

This principle implies that all parts of the body should contribute toward the desired objective. For example, in running, the body should lean forward slightly to contribute to the forward progress. In throwing, the total body should be used to exert the force, not just the arm and shoulder. All unnecessary movements should be eliminated. In running, the arms should not move across the body but should reach forward and pull backward. However, they should not reach forward or pull backward to an extreme position which will not contribute to the desired objective. The hands should be relaxed and not waste effort by being tense.

## Principle of Follow-through

When the desired movement is not completed, the previous action will not meet the intended objective. The power will fail and the accuracy will be effected. Therefore, it is necessary to be sure that the desired action is done to its completion. Reach for the target, give with the ball, and lift are cues to aide the performer in remembering to complete the skill.

## ELEMENTS OF MOVEMENT

### Space Elements

The area around us is space. We move through it with fundamental nonlocomotor and locomotor movements experiencing our relationship to space, which involves the following elements:

*Direction* is the external relationship of the body movements to space—left, right, forward, backward, diagonal, up, down, straight, curved, or spiral. The development of an understanding of directionality follows the understanding of laterality, which is the inner sense of directionality, left side and right side.

*Range* is the size of the movements. It includes the adjustment of the movement to the space and the desired objective of the movement.

*Dimension* refers to the size of the moving body or body part. The size of the body movement should meet the purpose of the movement efficiently.

*Focus* should be on the object or objective involved, whether it be for the purpose of striking or dodging.

*Design* is the pattern of the movement in space. Geometric shapes are a part of many physical activities.

*Level* is the height of the movement. The level of the body should be an appropriate height for successful execution of the movement. For example, the angle of an efficient crouch start for a short race can be achieved only by placing the body in the proper level for takeoff.

## Movement Quality

The basic elements of quality in movement indicate the different ways in which energy may be released, such as quick, slow, strong, or light. These elements may be combined to include various types of movements. Several are listed below:

*Sustained* movement is that with an even, moderate release of energy.

*Collapse* is a slow, light, relaxation movement.

*Swinging* is a slow, light, pendular movement.

*Striking* is a quick, strong, percussive movement.

*Dodging* is a quick, light, elusive movement.

The various basic movements most commonly used are categorized into two types—nonlocomotor and locomotor. In the following presentation the basic movement or skill is defined and some sample activities are listed.

## ACTIVITIES IN PLACE

There are many children who are limited extensively in their ability to move. These children are in need of directed physical activity which helps them to learn how to use their bodies. The following presentation contains a number of nonlocomotor activities which encourage a variety of movement to be learned. This is not intended to be a prescriptive approach for children with severe motor handicaps, but rather a presentation of movement activities which may be done by these children to provide for the development of normal physical skills. The activities are listed in progressive order from simple tasks to more complex tasks. Those activities listed are only a few of the possible movements and combinations of movements which may be given to the children to encourage the use of their bodies. From these ideas, the teacher may enlarge the list of movements to meet the needs of each individual.

## Teaching Suggestions

The following are suggestions for the teacher presenting non-locomotor activities:

1. When first presenting the task, it may be more beneficial for the child if the teacher actually moves the child through the desired motion. The child may then understand better how to do the activity.

2. Encourage the child to use the kinesthetic sense by which we feel the body moving. This will help the child to realize how the motion should be done. Ask him how it feels when he does the activity, and encourage him to try to repeat that feeling. It may help to have the child close his eyes in order to concentrate better on the "feeling" of the motion.

3. Any degree of success should be recognized and improvement encouraged. This contributes to the child's motivation for participation and better performance.

4. Be sure the action continues through the complete range of motion in the body joints. Big and vigorous movements are better than timid, restricted attempts.

5. Encourage the child to show what he can do by asking him to perform; for example, "Can you move your arms?" This will help the child to initiate the activity and show the teacher what actions the child knows. The teacher should then supplement the child's actions with actions done by other children or the teacher and thereby give the child added tasks to learn.

6. The children should be encouraged to name the parts of the body as they are used and verbalize in any other way the concepts they are learning.

7. Relate concepts learned by the children in their classroom experiences to the activities they are doing. This will help the children to understand better what the concepts mean to them as they use them in activities in which they are involved.

## Suggested Activities

### *Back Lying Position—Identification of Body Parts*

The teacher may use the following instructions and questions:

1. Touch your head.

 2. Touch your legs.
 3. Where are your arms?
 4. Show me your feet and your hands.
 5. Where is your elbow, knee, ankle?
 6. Do you have a hip?
 7. Move your fingers.
 8. Wiggle your thumb.
 9. Where are your toes and your heel?

### Back Lying Position—Movement Problems

Instructions and questions for use by the teacher are listed below:

 1. Cross your arms so your elbows touch.
 2. Move your arms away from your body.
 3. Move your feet apart.
 4. Reach toward the ceiling with your hands.
 5. Press your wrists against the floor and move your arms in an arc until you can clap your hands above your head.
 6. How far can you reach to your right with your right arm?
 7. How far can you reach to your left with your left arm?
 8. Lift your right leg as high as you can.
 9. Bend your left knee and place your left foot flat on the floor.
 10. Lift your right arm and your right leg as high as you can.
 11. Can you bend your right arm and left leg at the same time?
 12. Stretch your left arm and right leg.
 13. Move your arms quickly.
 14. Show me how big you can be.
 15. Stretch hard and relax (Check for relaxation and help the child to realize a relaxed position.)

### Facedown or Prone Position

Instructions are as follows:

 1. Point your toes toward the ceiling.
 2. Lift your arm as high as you can.
 3. Move your feet apart.
 4. Raise your right leg.
 5. What can you do with your head?

### Side Lying Position

The questions are listed below:
1. Can you become round like a ball?
2. What can you do with your right hand?
3. What can you do with your right leg?
4. What can you do with your right hand and right leg?
5. Can you make a circle?
6. What numbers can you make?
7. What letters can you make?
8. Show me how you can roll.

### Sitting Position

The questions are as follows:
1. What can you do with your feet and legs?
2. What can you do with your arms and hands?
3. Can you make a "V"?
4. Can you make a bridge?
5. Can you balance on two parts of your body?

### Kneeling Position

Instructions and questions follow:
1. Show me how many parts of your body you can shake.
2. Swing your arms.
3. Can you make a question mark?
4. Collapse to the floor.
5. Look like an angry cat.
6. What can you do while you balance on one knee?
7. Can you balance on three parts of your body?
8. Can you make a square, diamond, triangle, or a circle?
9. Can you crawl like a soldier?
10. How much space can you use?

### Standing Position

The questions are listed below:
1. Can you jump in place—with your feet together, with your feet apart, with one foot forward and one foot behind?
2. Can you turn around?

3. How big can you be?

4. How small can you be?

5. Can you stand on one foot?

6. Can you stand on one foot with your eyes closed?

7. Stand on one foot and explore what you can do with your other foot.

8. What can you do with one foot and one hand?

9. Can you make the letters of the alphabet?

10. What kind of shadows can you make? (This will need to be done in the sunlight or with a lamp behind the children.)

## NONLOCOMOTOR SKILLS

### Bend and Stretch

In bending movements, the body parts flex toward each other (Fig. 2-1). A stretching movement is the extending of the body parts (Fig. 2-2).

*Teaching Cues.* Stretching and bending activities should be done to include the full range of movement which will provide for good flexibility in the body joints. These actions may be done

Figure 2-1                          Figure 2-2

in a sitting, lying, or standing position, according to the child's ability and his need for variety.

*Precaution.* Avoid hyperextension of the knees and elbows. Do not bend the knee while supporting the body weight to a full squat position. This will cause extreme pressure to the knee joint.

### Suggested Activities

The following are questions and instructions for use in teaching bending and stretching movements:

1. How many parts of the body can you bend?
2. Bend all parts of the body until you are like a ball.
3. Bend the arms and legs toward the body.
4. Stretch and become as big as you can.
5. Bend and stretch the various parts of the body as they are named—arm, leg, body, neck, elbow, knee, wrist, ankle.
6. Can you bend your legs and stretch your arms?
7. Bend one arm and stretch the other arm.
8. Stretch to see how tall you can be.
9. Stretch like a puppy that just woke up.
10. How small can you be?

### Twist and Turn

In a twisting movement the body or body part rotates around a stationary base of support (Fig. 2-3). In a turning motion the base of support rotates with the body (Fig. 2-4).

*Teaching Cues.* While doing turning activities, focus on one spot in front of the area, keeping the eyes on that spot as long as possible and returning the focus of the eyes back to that spot as soon as possible.

Figure 2-3                    Figure 2-4

## *Suggested Activities*

The following are questions and instructions for use in teaching twisting and turning movements:

1. How many parts of the body can you twist?
2. Turn and face the side wall.
3. Turn and face the wall behind you.
4. Do a three-quarter turn.
5. Turn all the way around.
6. Turn the other way.
7. Twist the parts of the body as they are named.
8. Turn like a top using one foot.
9. Dance "beautifully" with lots of turns.
10. Twist your neck like you were a tall giraffe trying to see over the fence at the zoo.

## Rise and Fall

Rising is the upward motion from a low level (Fig. 2-5). Falling is the downward movement of the body or body parts from a higher level (Fig. 2-6).

Figure 2-5                                   Figure 2-6

*Teaching Cues.* Any time an individual participates in an activity, there is the possibility of falling. Everyone should be taught to fall correctly to avoid injury. Land on the musclar parts of the body—the shoulders, hips, and thighs. Keep the knees, hands, elbows, and head tucked for protection. Relax and roll in a curled position to absorb the momentum of the fall. Learn the fall and recovery from a low level and progress to an upright position.

*Note.* By using the continuous rolling motion of a fall, one can rise to an upward position and continue in the activity. The arms may help in the recovery. Football players use this technique. See illustrations (Figs. 2-7, 2-8, 2-9, 2-10).

<table>
<tr><td>Figure 2-7</td><td>Figure 2-8</td></tr>
</table>

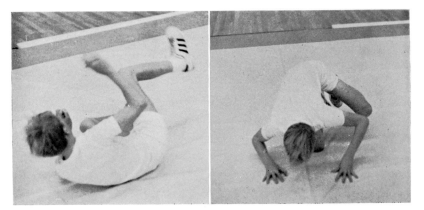

<table>
<tr><td>Figure 2-9</td><td>Figure 2-10</td></tr>
</table>

### Suggested Activities

The following are questions and instructions for use in teaching rising and falling movements:

1. Can you rise up from a sitting position to a standing position quickly?

2. Show how you get up out of bed in the morning.

3. From a sitting position, fall to the side by slowly relaxing. Land on the side and shoulder.

4. From a kneeling position, gradually fall to the side, rolling from the hip to the shoulder.

5. From a standing position, relax and fall to the side, rolling from the side of the thigh to the hip and shoulder.

6. Fall, roll, and recover to a standing position.

7. Pretend you are a flower seed which grows to be a beatutiful flower and then withers and dies in the hot sun.

8. Drop dead as if you were a cowboy who had just been shot.

9. Show how the sun rises in the morning and sets in the evening.

10. Show what a balloon does when you let go of it after you blow it up.

11. Burst like a balloon that has just popped.

12. Melt like an ice cream cone.

### Swing and Sway

A swing is a pendular movement in which the base of support is above the moving body part (Fig. 2-11). In a swaying movement the base of support is below the moving part (Fig. 2-12).

*Suggested Activities*

The following are questions and instructions for use in teaching swinging and swaying movements:

1. How many parts of the body can you sway while standing up?

2. How many parts of the body can you sway while lying on your back?

3. Swing as many parts of the body as you can.

4. Show how you swing at a baseball and at a golf ball.

5. Sway like a tree does when the breeze blows briskly.

6. Swing your arms and see how high you can jump.

7. Swing your arms together and in opposition.

8. Swing your leg as if you were kicking a football.

Figure 2-11

Figure 2-12

9. Swing your arms like the pendulum of a cuckoo clock.
10. Sway with the rhythm of the record.
11. Sway from the back foot to the front foot as you throw a ball.

### Strike and Dodge

A strike is a percussive movement toward an object (Fig. 2-13). A dodge is an elusive movement away from an object or person (Fig. 2-14).

*Teaching Cues.* The children should be encouraged to use the whole body when imparting force to an object. When teaching the children how to dodge, remind them to keep their knees bent, thus keeping the center of gravity low, to use the arms for balance, and to push off from the supporting foot or feet. To be able to move in any direction, they should keep the weight on both feet in a good ready position.

Figure 2-13                    Figure 2-14

## *Suggested Activities*

The following are instructions and questions for use in teaching striking and dodging movements:

1. Dodge an immaginary ball thrown at your waist.
2. Show what a tetherball game looks like.
3. How many different ways can you strike a ball?
4. Pretend someone is chasing you and dodge him.
5. Show how you chop down a tree.
6. Play bean-bag dodge.
7. Slash your way through a forest.
8. Run through an obstacle course without touching anything.
9. Duck to dodge an object.
10. Jump to dodge an object.

### Push and Pull

Pushing is directing force away from the body (Fig. 2-15). Pulling is directing force toward the body (Fig. 2-16).

*Precaution.* When pushing or pulling an object or another person, it is important to lower the center of gravity by bending the knees and to use the leg muscles to direct the force. The body should be on a slight incline toward the direction of the force.

Figure 2-15

Figure 2-16

*Suggested Activities*

The following are instructions for use in teaching pushing and pulling movements:

1. Grasp right hands with a partner and pull him across a line.

2. Grasp left hands with a partner and pull him across a line.

3. Use a two-hand grip and try to pull a partner across a line.

4. Stand back to back with a partner and try to push him until he moves his feet.

5. Place your hands on your partner's back and push until one of you moves your feet.

6. Have a tug-of-war with the class. Use correct pulling technique.

7. Pull a wagon with several items in it.

8. Push an object. Use the correct technique.

9. Sit down back to back with a partner. Try to push him over a line.

10. Grasp right hands with a partner. Push and pull without moving your feet until he moves his feet.

## LOCOMOTOR SKILLS

### Walk

A walk is a transfer of weight from one foot to the other foot, with one foot always in contact with the floor (Fig. 2-17).

*Teaching Cues.* In moving through space, the child should use good walking technique, assume good posture with the head erect and the chest lifted, point the feet forward, use proper transfer of weight from the heel along the outside of the foot and across the ball of the foot, and push off with the toes.

*Suggested Activities*

The following are instructions and questions for use in teaching walking movements:

1. Walk forward, backward, to the right, to the left, and on a diagonal.

2. Walk and freeze on the signal. Hold your balance.

3. Walk heavily, lightly, quietly, and noisily.

4. Walk low, and on your tip toes; change position on the signal.

5. Walk with big steps, giant steps, and small steps.

6. Show how you walk when you are happy, angry, afraid, tired, on ice, in the wind, and in the rain.

7. How many body parts can you move while you are walking?

8. Walk like an elephant, a tiger, a horse, and so forth.

9. Can you walk quickly, and then slowly?

10. Have a walking race. (Be sure the children do a walk, not a run.)

11. Walk through the space without touching anyone else. The area will gradually get smaller. Remember correct procedures for dodging.

### Run

The movement of a run is a walk, with the exception that there is a time when both feet are off the floor (Fig. 2-18).

Figure 2-17                              Figure 2-18

*Teaching Cues.* All movements should be toward the direction of the run, usually forward. Sideward movement should be discouraged. Look forward with the head up.

All body parts should contribute to the desired movement. A slight body lean forward will help move the body weight forward. The body lean should increase when more speed is desired. The arms, with the elbows bent, should move forward so the hands are shoulder high and backward until the hands are next to the hip.

The leg action is initiated from the hip. The knee lift depends on the speed of the run. When jogging, little knee lift is needed. When running for speed, a high knee lift is used.

Land on the balls of the feet and "toe down" to the heel.

*Note.* Some children with restricted movement run with a flat foot. These children can be taught to run correctly by progressing from a walk on the toes, with a "toe down" action using the ankle, to a run landing lightly on the balls of the feet.

## Suggested Activities

The following are instructions for use in teaching running movements:

1. Jog around the area.
2. Run and stop on the signal. Use only two steps to stop.
3. Run in the area without touching anyone. The area will become smaller.
4. Run with a long stride or big steps.
5. Run with short, quick steps.
6. Keep running and change direction as the command is given to go forward, backward, to the right, to the left, and reverse.
7. Run low and gradually get higher and higher.
8. Run through an obstacle course without touching anything.
9. Run like you are trying to hide.
10. Run as fast as you can and as slowly as you can.

**Leap**

The leap is a movement through space with a transfer of weight from one foot to the other foot, during which the body is elevated and suspended in the air for an extended length of time (Fig. 2-19). It is an extended run.

Figure 2-19

*Teaching Cues.* The arms should help lift and reach in opposition (right arm and left leg forward) to help sustain the movement.

### Suggested Activities

The following are questions and instructions for use in teaching leaping movements:

1. How far can you leap?
2. How high can you leap?
3. Leap five times in a row.
4. Leap with the left leg leading.
5. Leap with the right leg leading.
6. Run two steps and leap.
7. Run with a partner and leap together.

8. Leap and reach as high as you can.
9. Can you do several leaps quickly?
10. Use as much space as you can as you leap.

## Jump

A jump is a transfer of weight from one or both feet to both feet simultaneously (Figs. 2-20A and 2-20B).

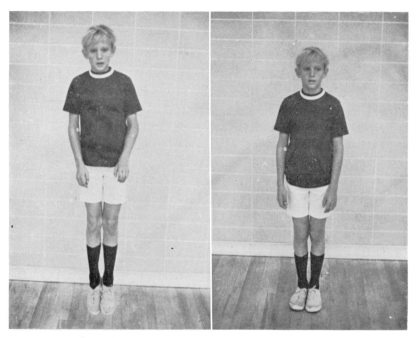

Figure 2-20A                              Figure 2-20B

*Teaching Cues.* Bend the ankles, knees, and hips in preparation for the jump. Swing the arms from behind the hips upward in the direction of the jump. This will help move the body. When landing, bend the hips, knees, and ankles to absorb the movement.

### Suggested Activities

The following are questions and instructions for use in teaching jumping movements:

1. Can you jump high and land lightly?
2. Can you jump and turn around?
3. Jump and reach as high as you can.
4. Jump forward, backward, and sideward.
5. Run several steps and jump.
6. How far can you jump?
7. Jump like a kangaroo.
8. Can you jump several times quickly?
9. Jump as high as you can.

## Hop

A hop is a transfer of weight from one foot to the same foot (Fig. 2-21).

*Teaching Cues.* Swing the arms to gain more momentum. When landing, give with the knee and ankle. Keep the free foot off the floor.

### Suggested Activities

The following are instructions and questions for use in teaching hopping movements:

1. Hop on the right foot.
2. Hop on the left foot.
3. How high can you hop?
4. How far can you hop?
5. Can you hop and turn around?
6. Hop forward, backward, and to the right and left.
7. Hop three times on the left foot and three times on the right foot.
8. Hop as quickly as you can.
9. Hop and swing the arms.
10. Take as few hops as possible to cover twenty feet.

## Skip

A skip is a combination of a walk and a hop, with an uneven rhythm and with elevation (Fig. 2-22). The foot pattern is a step right, hop right, step left, hop left. The rhythm is a slow (step), quick (hop) uneven pattern.

Figure 2-21                                    Figure 2-22

*Teaching Cues.* Swing the arms in opposition. Also, the mood while skipping is usually one of joy or happiness. Land lightly.

### Suggested Activities

The following are instructions for use in teaching skipping movements:

1. Skip high
2. Skip low.
3. Skip fast.
4. Skip and turn around.
5. Be as big as you can while you skip.
6. Skip forward, backward, to the right, and to the left.
7. Move as many parts of your body as you can while you skip.
8. Skip and make a circle, a square, or a diamond.
9. Skip quietly and then loudly.
10. Take as few skips as possible to go from one line to another line.

## Slide

In order to slide, step to the side, move the other foot to meet the supporting foot, and transfer weight (Fig. 2-23). The movement is an uneven one—slow (step), quick (leap to the free foot).

*Teaching Cues.* Use the arms to help by swinging them slightly during the transfer of weight. Land lightly.

### Suggested Activities

The following are instructions and questions for use in teaching sliding movements:

1. Slide with a long step.
2. How high can you go while you slide?
3. Can you slide down low?
4. Make a triangle while you slide in your own area.
5. Do something new while you slide.
6. Slide with a partner, face to face and back to back.
7. Be as big as you can while you slide.
8. Slide forward, backward, and to the side.
9. Slide as quickly as you can from one line to another line.
10. In a circle holding hands with the group, slide eight steps

to the right and eight steps to the left. Slide four steps to the right and four steps to the left. Slide two steps to the right and two steps to the left. Continue to slide two steps to the right and two steps to the left and turn to face the direction of the slide. The group is now doing a polka—hop, step close step.

## Gallop

A gallop is a movement like a slide, done while moving forward (Fig. 2-24). The pattern of the movement is as follows: a step forward on one foot, move the other foot to meet the supporting foot, and transfer the weight to the back foot with a leap.

*Teaching Cues.* The same leg always leads the movement, and the rhythm is an uneven movement—slow (step), quick (transfer to the back foot). Land lightly.

Figure 2-23          Figure 2-24

### Suggested Activities

The following are instructions for use in teaching galloping movements:

1. Gallop forward.
2. Gallop as fast as you can.
3. Gallop as high as you can.
4. Gallop like a pony.
5. Gallop like a prancing circus horse.
6. While you gallop, do tricks with your arms.
7. Gallop like an old mule.
8. Gallop like a work horse.
9. Gallop in a circle.
10. Gallop and jump a ditch.

## MOVEMENT EXPLORATION ACTIVITIES

### Space Exploration

The following are instructions and questions for use in teaching space exploration activities:

1. Explore your own space, always keeping one foot or one hand on the ground. How big is it? How high is it?

2. Explore two objects in the area and return to your own spot.

3. Hop to a corner in the room and skip back to your spot.

4. How fast can you run around the area and return to your spot?

5. Explore the ceiling and the walls and report what you saw to the teacher.

### Partner Activities

The following are instructions for use in teaching movement exploration activities with partners:

1. Jump over your partner.

2. Be a seesaw with your partner and rise and fall in opposition.

3. Make a bridge so your partner can go under and over it.

4. Do the different locomotor movements with your partner.

5. Have your partner count while you hop five times on each foot.

### Group Activities

The following are instructions for use in teaching group movement exploration activities:

1. Follow the leader, who will do the various locomotor and nonlocomotor skills.

2. Form a circle. Skip ten steps away from the circle and run back to the circle.

3. Every other person in the circle weave in and out of the remaining members of the circle. Walk at first, then run.

4. Slide in a circle and then gallop.

5. As a group make the various geometric shapes.

### Action Words and Pictures

The following are instructions for use with action words and pictures:

1. Do the actions shown in the pictures. (Show pictures of children running, playing ball, riding horses, and so forth.)

2. Mimic the actions of the objects in the pictures. (Show pictures of airplanes, trains, birds, elephants, Indians dancing, and so on.)

3. Do the actions of the words on the flash cards. (Use words like "vibrate," "ouch," "crash," "shake," "sigh," "laugh," "oh," "fall." These words may need to be illustrated on the card for some children.)

4. Make the shape shown on the picture. (The cards may have numbers, letters, or geometric shapes.)

5. As the teacher tells the story, every time you hear the action words or key words, do the action and then listen to the story for another action word. (Tell a story like "Going through the Jungle." The action words should be repeated often in the story. "Fall," "shiver," "crash," and so on are good action words.)

## Drama Activities

The following are instructions and questions for use in drama activities:

1. Show how you feel when it is raining on you.
2. How does the sun make you feel?
3. What does the color green make you do?
4. Show how grandmother walks.
5. Are you sad or happy? Show me.
6. What do you do when you are angry?
7. How do you feel after a race?
8. Show what your favorite baseball star or football star can do.
9. Can you dance like a ballerina?
10. Can you roll like a ball or wheel? Can you push like a bulldozer?
11. Do pantomimes and see if the class can guess what you are doing.
12. Use only your actions and expressions to tell a story.
13. Be a circus performer.
14. What do you do on New Year's Day?

# Chapter 3

# MOVEMENT EXPLORATION USING EQUIPMENT

Movement exploration using various pieces of equipment allows freedom of expression often never dreamed of by the manufacturers of the equipment. Children are very able to experiment, imitate, and make up new activities to do with toys or equipment. A retarded child will need a structured experience for a while when being introduced to new equipment. He will want and need suggestions as to what to do. He eventually will feel familiar enough with the equipment that he will create, experiment, and even teach new and different ways to use the equipment. He then will be benefiting in a creative way from participating in the activity, and will be thinking, acting, and enjoying the experience.

The teacher should plan to teach the children how to use the equipment, and she should include several things which can be done with the equipment before she turns the children freely over to experimentation. She should remain in charge of the activity, and the children should not be allowed to become unruly. They should be under control at all times. She can say, "Let's all do what John is doing," or, "Show the class, Sue, what you can do."

The equipment used in this chapter is inexpensive and readily available. Some of the activities are group activities and some are individual. Exploration of the equipment can be a lesson in itself or can be a pace changer at the end of another lesson in physical education. After the children are familiar with its use, some of the equipment can be a special treat as a reward for something really great that has been displayed by the class. The activities presented are suggested to get the task started. The list for each piece of equipment is limitless.

## PARACHUTES

Activities using the parachute provide the child with an opportunity for group experience. The entire group must work together toward the common goal of various stunts or games. Parachutes are available for about thirty dollars at military surplus stores or through the purchasing agent in the school. They come in many colors and are appealing to the children. They should be stored in a bag or a box so that they will not get dirty or torn.

1. Children take a two-hand hold around the edge of the parachute. On the signal "Up," all of the children lift the parachute by pulling up and allowing the chute to billow upward (Fig. 3-1). On the signal "Down," all of the children pull the chute down toward the floor. Keep repeating "Up" and "Down." The children should all work together to control the parachute.

Figure 3-1

2. One child sits in the center of the chute. The other children, with no signal other than "Go," shake the parachute up and down rapidly. The chute tends to surround the child who is sitting in the center (Fig. 3-2).

Figure 3-2

3. The children take a two-hand hold around the edge of the parachute. Everyone pulls out on the parachute and leans back (Fig. 3-3). The children on one side of the chute lift the chute and then lower it while the children on the other side are lifting.

Figure 3-3

4. Children do number 3 with a ball placed in the chute. The ball will roll around the circle on the chute as the chute is lowered.

5. Children raise the chute with a ball placed in the center. The ball is to be snapped into the air by the chute and caught by the chute in time to be snapped again.

Figure 3-4

Figure 3-5

6. The children raise the chute. The teacher calls the names of two children as the chute is almost full of air. When the chute is filled the two children exchange places by running under the chute before it falls to the floor (Fig. 3-4).

7. The children raise the chute. Two children at a time are selected to get under the parachute. As the chute begins to lower the children on the outside force the chute to the floor. The children under the chute attempt to get out from under the chute while the children on the outside try to keep them in (Fig. 3-5).

## HOOPS

The hoop has been a toy of childhood through history. The hoop that is made of brightly colored plastic is inexpensive and available in any toy store. The activities with the hoop offer experiments in combining tumbling, jumping, crawling, rolling, throwing, catching, and spinning.

1. Children jump the hoop like a jump rope (Fig. 3-6).

2. One child rolls the hoop to a partner (Fig. 3-7).

Figure 3-6

Figure 3-7

3. One child rolls the hoop to a partner and a third child rolls a ball through the hoop to a partner.

4. One child puts a backspin on the hoop; at the moment the hoop starts to roll back, a child crawls through the hoop (Fig. 3-8).

5. Children each hold a hoop and form a circle—child, hoop, child, hoop. Another child runs in and out the windows by running through the hoop into and out of the circle (Fig. 3-9).

6. Number 5 can be a tag game if two children are used and if the children need a competitive experience.

7. The child spins the hoop on various parts of the body—leg, arm, neck, waist, or knees (Fig. 3-10).

### TIRES

Activities using automobile tires provide a strenuous, rugged type of experience. Football players work out doing some exercise with tires. Tires are available for the asking from garage and service station owners, and from some car owners. The tires should be scrubbed, dried, and then painted bright colors.

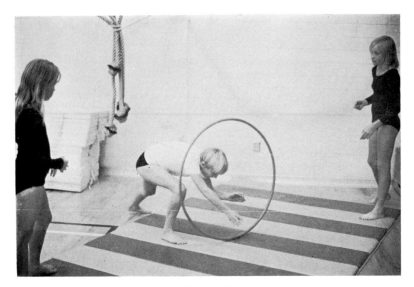

Figure 3-8

Figure 3-9

Figure 3-10

1. *Leg Strength Run.* Place the tires in two adjacent and touching rows. The child runs down the rows placing one foot in each tire. The child should run slowly at first to get used to the feeling of lifting the knees high enough so that the feet will clear the tires. This activity can be used as a relay race if the children need a competitive experience.

2. *Leapfrog.* The child stands behind the tire with his hands on the top of the tire. He rolls the tire toward him, straddle jumps over the tire, and lets it roll behind him.

3. *Jump Over.* One child rolls the tire to another child, who jumps over the tire as it rolls toward him.

4. *Walk Around.* The child stands on the tire facing in and walks around the tire by taking small side steps. This can also be done as a partner stunt with two children facing each other and holding hands as they walk around the tire.

5. *Target.* The tires can be used as targets into which bean bags may be thrown.

6. *Tunnel.* Stand the tires on end and side by side to form a tunnel. The children are the train cars and crawl through the tunnel. This can be used as a relay race if a competitive activity is needed.

## BALLS

Activities in ball handling have been included in other sections of the book and will not be repeated here. Exploration in movement using balls offers limitless opportunities for experimentation with balls of all sizes.

Figure 3-11

Figure 3-12

Figure 3-13

1. How high can the ball bounce?
2. How many times does the ball bounce?

3. How loud does the ball sound when it bounces?
4. How quietly can you make the ball bounce?
5. Can you spin the ball? (Fig. 3-11.)
6. Can you roll the ball down your arm? (Fig. 3-12.)
7. What can we do with this great big ball? (Fig. 3-13.)

### JUMPING BALLS

These balls have several brand names and are available at toy stores. They come in bright colors of blue, red, green, and yellow. It is necessary for each child in the group to have one on which to jump because the balls are so attractive and fun to use that sharing is not desirable.

Figure 3-14

The child sits on the ball and holds onto the handle in front of him (Fig. 3-14). He pushes with his feet and bounces. The teacher should allow the children free time on the balls. The children will soon be jumping and bouncing all over the room and will probably bump into each other. It is a good idea for the teacher to have a jumping ball also. This is one activity at which children do better than an adult, and the children will enjoy being a better performer than the teacher.

## ELASTIC BANDS

Elastic bands are made from two yards of elastic braid with the ends sewed together to form a ring. The activities are exercise in nature and they allow freedom of movement that is not readily available in a formal exercise program.

1. The child is in a long sitting position with the elastic band around both ankles. The child separates the feet, keeping the legs straight and stretching the elastic (Fig. 3-15).

2. The child is in a long sitting position with the elastic band around both wrists. The child separates the hands, keeping the arms straight and stretching the elastic (Fig. 3-16).

3. The child is in a long sitting position with the elastic band around one ankle and the wrist on the same side. The child raises the arm and stretches the elastic (Fig. 3-17). Alternate sides.

Figure 3-15

4. The child is in a long sitting position with the elastic around one ankle and the opposite wrist. The child raises the arm and twists, stretching the body (Fig. 3-18).

5. The child is in a long sitting position with the elastic around both ankles. The child attempts to stand up without the elastic band falling off the ankles (Fig. 3-19).

Figure 3-16

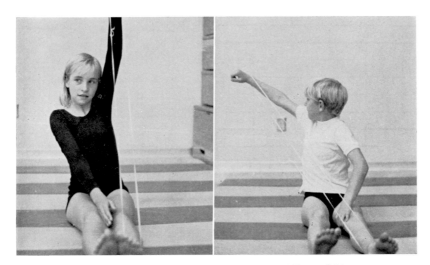

Figure 3-17                                  Figure 3-18

6. The child is in a long sitting position with the elastic band around one ankle and one wrist. The child attempts to stand without the elastic band falling off (Fig. 3-20).

Figure 3-19

Figure 3-20

## OBSTACLE COURSES

Included in this chapter on movement exploration is material on obstacle courses because the older children can make up obstacle courses that they would like to run and these courses can be an enriching addition to the physical education program. An obstacle course provides strenuous activity in a creative and fun manner. The course should include a variety of activities and changes of level. The equipment used in the equipment-type obstacle courses is available around any school situation.

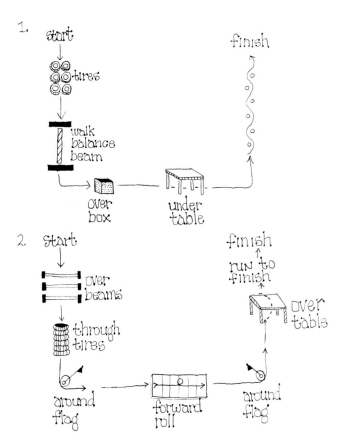

3.

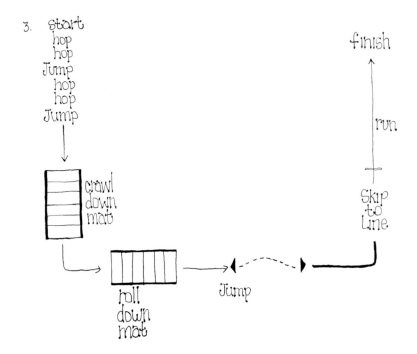

# Chapter 4

# MOTOR-PERCEPTUAL ACTIVITIES

An INDIVIDUAL can perform mentally only as well as he feels physically. If poor health or lack of physical fitness do not provide the energy to participate willingly, the children are not able to apply themselves to the academic pursuit. Likewise, if he has no confidence in his ability, he will be at a disadvantage academically. Success in performing physical skills and games helps the child to approach all tasks more willingly. Therefore, it is important that a child has a good image of himself and his ability to succeed. Physical activities provide the child with considerable feedback concerning his ability. The movement exploration section of this text is an excellent means to provide for the development of a good body image. Movement exploration activities are good from a developmental standpoint and also provide for a measure of success for each child regardless of his limitations.

In addition to providing an atmosphere for learning, physical activities extend an opportunity for the development of the necessary perceptual skills in a more involved, yet less stressful, setting. Learning results from the awareness of our environment. This awareness is accomplished by the perceptual abilities a child possesses. The more able his perceptual abilities are, the more learning he will achieve. Our physical senses—visual, auditory, and kinesthetic—provide the tools we use in perceiving our environment, and through physical activity the use of these senses may be practiced and improved. In the activities presented in the other chapters of the text, the use of visual, auditory, and kinesthetic senses has been encouraged and practiced; in some cases, specifically designed activities have been presented to develop the use of these senses. To be specific, visual perception is practiced in activities such as rope jumping, ball handling, bean-bag activities, equipment exploration, and stunts and tumbling. Auditory perception is used in the verbalization of the ball skills, low-organization games, and the rhythms in movement exploration. Kinesthetic perception is practiced in all activity. Each type of motor development is listed below with the activities which contribute most to this type of development:

*Laterality* is developed by movement exploration, balance beam, rhythms, marching, aquatics, ball skills, and conditioning exercises.

*Directionality* develops from movement exploration, balance beam, ball skills, and rhythms.

*Body image* is improved by trampoline work, stunts and tumbling, games, movement exploration, and equipment exploration.

*Coordination* improves with movement exploration, ball skills, conditioning exercises, stunts and tumbling, and games.

The activities presented in the following section were created with the development of perceptual skills as the specific purpose of the activity. These are only a few examples of dual-purpose activities. They demonstrate how many common physical activities can be adapted to meet the need for development of perceptual-motor skills and academic concepts.

## Teaching Suggestions

The following are some suggestions for the teaching of perceptual-motor skills:

1. Encourage the child to verbalize the color, shape, or size of the object he uses.

2. Repeat the task several times to reinforce the learned concept. Then vary the pattern so the child will begin to discern the variation in size, shape, or color.

3. Do not combine the various projects, such as numbers or colors, until each type of concept is well learned.

### *Color Discrimination*

Listed below are activities for use in teaching color discrimination skills:

1. Place several colored patches of oil cloth, a variety of sizes, around the room. Have the children go to a blue patch, red patch, and so on until all the colors have been used.

2. Place several colored targets on the walls. On command, direct the children to go to each color and touch it.

3. Have the children throw a ball at a colored target and verbally indicate the color of the target.

4. Have each child select a ball from a box of colored balls and throw it at the colored target which is the same color as the ball he selected.

5. Place a set of different colored patches in a row in front of a line of children. A colored block for each patch is placed on the starting line. Each child, in turn, takes one block and places it on the matching colored patch. The task may be changed so the children place the colored blocks on different colored patches as the teacher names them.

6. Have the children throw the big balls at the big targets and the small balls at the small targets.

### Size Differentiation

*Preparation.* Place before the children an oil-cloth chart or charts on which diamonds, rectangles, triangles, and circles have been painted (Fig. 4-1). There should be several of each shape, with each having a different number, size, and color than the others of the same shape. The children should have a set of patches to match the shapes, colors, sizes, and numbers on the chart.

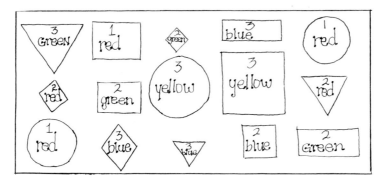

Figure 4-1

1. Have each child, in turn, run from a starting line to the chart with a patch in his hand and place the patch on the chart so that shape matches.

2. Have the children hop to the chart with a patch and match the shape and size of the patch with the same design on the chart.

3. As the children jump to the chart, name the shape on which the children should stand.

4. Have each child, in turn, run to the maze, stand on a design, and name the shape on which he is standing.

5. Have the children match the colors as well as the shape of the patches on the chart.

6. Call out a color and have the children stand on a design of that color.

7. Have the children match the size, shape, and color of the patches with a design on the chart.

8. Tell the children to match the number on the patch with the number on the chart.

9. Have the children match the shape and number of the patch with the proper design on the chart.

10. Have each child place the patch on the chart so the size, shape, color, and number match.

11. Place the patches in scattered formation on the floor. As the teacher names the shape, size, number, and/or color, the children run to the appropriate patch.

12. As a class, have the children play follow-the-leader and make the different geometric shapes, with the class members forming the designs.

13. Have each child make a design with his body while lying on the floor.

14. Have the children crawl through boxes in which the holes are cut in the various geometric shapes.

### Auditory Differentiation

The following activities are useful in teaching auditory differentiation skills:

1. As the children are running freely in the area, give a com-

mand or blow a whistle on which the children "freeze" immediately.

2. Play a series of recorded sounds which represent typical sounds in the child's environment. Help the children recognize the sound and do the activity which the sound represents, such as a train, a dog, or a soldier.

3. Beat a drum to various rhythms to which the children hop, walk, and so forth.

4. As the instruments make the various sounds, have the children do the movements represented by the sounds, such as tambourine—dance, shakers—shake, tuning fork—vibrate, and so on.

5. With the children's eyes closed, tap a beat pattern and have the children hop out the pattern.

### Visual Discrimination and Kinesthetic Awareness

Activities for use in teaching these skills are listed below:

1. Have the children mirror the activity done by the teacher. Start with gross movements, such as running in place, and progress to fine motor movements, such as finger patterns.

2. Set up a circuit with stations around the area. As the whistle blows, have the children progress to the next station and do the exercise which is drawn on the chart until the whistle blows again.

3. Have the children close their eyes and touch the parts of their body as they are named.

4. Start each child on a line and have the child walk on the line.

5. Have the children walk in the area without stepping on a line or crack.

6. Have the children mirror a position demonstrated by the teacher—a scarecrow and so forth. Next have them close their eyes and assume the same position.

7. Have the children throw a ball at a target with their eyes closed.

8. Direct the children to jump over a taped line approximately two feet apart. Have them repeat the task with their eyes closed.

9. Have the children do different locomotor movements through mazes placed on the floor (Fig. 4-2).

10. Use the hopscotch maze on the playground at school and design a movement pattern for the children to follow (Fig. 4-3).

11. Play hopscotch.

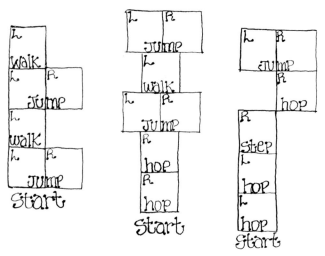

Figure 4-2

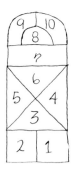

Figure 4-3

# Chapter 5

# EXERCISE THEORY AND PRACTICE

HANDICAPPED CHILDREN have the same need for exercise that normal people have. Enthusiasm and ambition are necessary qualities for enjoyment and success in life's endeavors. These qualities depend greatly on the vigor and energy our physical condition provides. It is through use that the physical systems of the body function efficiently—lack of strength, poor circulation, sluggish reflexes, tenseness, atrophy, fatigue, and general poor health are results of inactivity. In many cases, physical handicaps such as poor posture and poor muscular and bone development result from a deficiency of physical activity.

To provide for a general feeling of good health and proper growth, it is essential that a regular program of exercise be designed for each child. The following presentation incorporates the theory of an exercise program and includes several exercises from which to select when designing an exercise program. The purpose of the exercises has been designed in terms of the type of physical development expected and the area of the body for which the exercise was constructed.

## COMPONENTS OF PHYSICAL FITNESS

Physical fitness is the ability to meet everyday occurrences succesfully with a reserve of energy for an emergency or recreational pursuit. In order to understand better the state of physical fitness and how it is obtained and retained, it is necessary to know the components of such a status.

*Strength.* The muscular power to resist force or move against force is termed strength. To increase strength, the degree of resistance applied to the working muscle must be increased. This may be done by adding an external weight or by a change of body position, thereby increasing the body weight to be moved in the exercise.

*Flexibility.* The range of motion in the body joints indicates the degree of flexibility in each area of the body. Exercises to obtain and maintain the normal range of motion are necessary to keep the body parts functioning efficiently and to insure good posture. Flexibility exercises should be performed before a strenous activity in order to prepare the muscles for movement.

*Endurance.* Muscular endurance is the ability of a muscle to continue to perform a task. Cardiorespiratory endurance is the ability of the respiratory and circulatory systems of the body to function efficiently and without stress in providing the muscles with the energy necessary to function. Increased breathing rate and heartbeat rate are responses to the energy needs of the working body parts. In a conditioned person the heart beat is slower, the circulation is better, the lungs have greater capacity, and the heart is more efficient. Therefore, they can be more effective in meeting the demands of the working areas of the body. Endurance exercises are usually performed near the need of an exercise period.

*Coordination.* The ability to move body parts willfully and efficiently toward a common goal is termed coordination. Practice of coordinated body movements enhances the ability to use learned motor patterns and to learn new movement patterns.

*Agility.* Agility is the ability to change body positions with grace and ease. Movement through various body positions as a practice exercise will help develop effective, coordinated body movements.

*Balance.* Balance is the ability to maintain a stable posture in various positions. Through practice, adjustment in body positions to maintain balance while moving through space can be learned.

## EXERCISE PROGRAMMING

In constructing a fitness exercise program, exercises designed to develop each of the components of physical fitness should be selected for the various areas of the body. The repetitions of each exercise performed will also depend on the purpose of the exercise. Strength exercises are usually performed a maximum of ten times. The work load or the resistance of the exercise is then changed to increase the strength required. As the work load is changed for an exercise, it becomes a new progression of the same exercise. When an exercise program is started, strength exercises should be repeated three times the first day, five times the second day, seven times the third day and ten times from there on until the progression is changed. This gradual approach will prevent extensive stiffness. Endurance exercises should become gradually more demanding by continually increasing the number of repetitions until the desired level of fitness is attained. Each day the cardiorespiratory system should be overloaded, thus gradually increasing the capacity and efficiency of the heart and lungs.

The exercises presented in this chapter have been selected for their known contribution toward physical fitness. The major contribution of each exercise and the general body area for which it was designed is designated. These exercises are "isotonic," or moving-type exercises. For most exercises, a basic four count is used to move into position, thereby providing continuous smooth movement. Each exercise should be held four counts, and four counts are used to return to the starting position. Strength exercises should be performed slowly and in a controlled manner. Endurance exercises can be done quickly and vigorously. Care should be taken to encourage a full range of motion in all exercises.

Isometric exercises provide variety in an exercise program. An isometric exercise is done by pushing vigorously against an external force in a static contraction for a six-second count. The various positions for isotonic exercises may be adapted to isometric exercises. The force may be one's own body part against another body part, a partner's resistance, or activities of resistance such as a tug-of-war.

## Exercises

### *Toe Touch (Standing Position)*

*Purpose.* Low-back and hamstring flexibility.

*Procedure.* Stand with the knees straight. Bend forward and hang the head and hands toward the toes. Stretch gently until a slight stretch pain is felt. (See Fig. 5-1.)

*Precaution.* Do not bounce. Keep the knees straight.

### Toe Touch (Sitting Position)

*Purpose.* Hamstring flexibility.

*Procedure.* Sit with the legs extended forward and the knees straight, the toes pointed and the arms forward. Reach the fingers toward the toes (Fig. 5-2), hold, and return to the starting position.

*Precaution.* Keep the knees straight. Do not bounce.

Figure 5-1                          Figure 5-2

### Airplane

*Purpose.* Low-back and hamstring flexibility.

*Procedure.* Stand with the feet shoulder-width apart. Hold the arms up and straight at shoulder level. On count one twist the upper body to the left and bend forward, reaching the right hand toward the left foot (Fig. 5-3). On count two return to an upright position and return to the starting position. Repeat the exercise to the right.

*Precaution.* As the hand reaches for the foot, be sure to rotate the trunk.

### Shoulder Stretch

*Purpose.* Shoulder flexibility.

*Procedure.* Hold a three-foot rope, wand, or towel near the ends. With the arms straight, move the towel from in front, up over the head, and behind the back (Fig. 5-4). Return back over the head to the starting position.

*Precaution.* Keep the arms straight. Move the hands closer together to provide more stretch.

Figure 5-3                Figure 5-4

### Heel Cord Stretch

*Purpose.* Lower-leg and ankle flexibility.

*Procedure.* Stand facing the wall, approximately two feet away. Place the hands on the wall at shoulder level. With the body straight, lean toward the wall and keep the heels on the floor (Fig. 5-5). For a greater stretch, stand further from the wall.

*Precaution.* Keep the hips and waist straight.

### Arm Circles

*Purpose.* Shoulder strength and flexibility.

*Procedure.* Hold the arms shoulder high and to the sides, palms upward (Fig. 5-6). Rotate the arms backward, making a circle with the arms. Make small circles, progressing to large circle in which the arms go backward and forward as far as possible.

*Precaution.* Keep the arms and back straight and the head erect.

Figure 5-5                    Figure 5-6

### Hands and Knees

*Purpose.* Abdominal strength.

*Procedure.* Kneel on the hands and knees with the knees directly under the hips and the hands under the shoulders. Relax the abdominal wall so that the back is arched and the head is up (Fig. 5-7). Make a hump with the lower back by dropping the head and contracting the abdominal muscles (Fig. 5-8). After holding this position for three to five seconds, relax the abdominal muscles, lift the head, and return to the starting position.

*Precaution.* Keep the arms straight and breath normally.

### Curl

*Purpose.* Abdominal strength.

*Procedure.* In a back lying position with the legs straight, place the hands on the thighs. Rotate the hips so that the small of

Figure 5-7

Figure 5-8

the back touches the floor. Lift the head and place the chin on the chest (Fig. 5-9). Slowly and smoothly lift the upper trunk in a curling motion until a sitting position is reached. Curl back down slowly. Second progression: With the knees bent, the feet flat on the floor and the hands reaching forward, curl to a sitting position in the manner described above (Fig. 5-10). Third progression: Lace the fingers behind the head, and with the legs straight, curl to a sitting position (Fig. 5-11). Fourth progression: With the hands behind the head and the knees bent, curl to a sitting position (Fig. 5-12).

*Precaution.* Keep the back rounded. Do not jerk up. Each progression should be performed ten times smoothly before proceeding to the next exercise position.

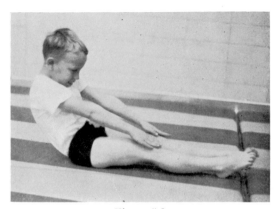

Figure 5-9

Figure 5-10

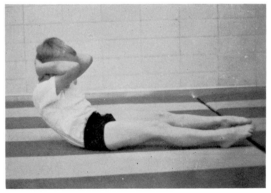

Figure 5-11

Figure 5-12

### Rotation Curl

*Purpose.* Abdominal strength.

*Procedure.* Begin the curl from a back lying position with one arm folded across the chest. As the upward curling motion begins, rotate by reaching toward the opposite knee with the free hand (Fig. 5-13). Return to the starting position by reversing the action. Alternate sides. The progressions for this exercise are the same as those listed for the curl exercise. When this exercise can be performed ten times, do the exercise as described in the second repetition of the curl with a rotation. Use the same procedure for the third and fourth progressions.

*Precaution.* Do not roll to the side. Lift and rotate smoothly.

### Bent-Knee Leg Lifts

*Purpose.* Lower-abdominal strength.

*Procedure.* From a back lying position with the small of the back flat on the floor, bend and lift the knees to the chest (Fig. 5-14). Return to the starting position.

*Precaution.* Bend the knees before lifting them to the chest.

### Modified Push-ups

*Purpose.* Arm and shoulder strength.

*Procedure.* Assume a straight-arm support position with the

Figure 5-13                    Figure 5-14

weight on the hands and the knees (Fig. 5-15). Lower the body until the chest touches the floor. Return to the starting position.

*Precaution.* Keep the body in a straight line by contracting the trunk and hip muscles. Do not arch the back. Keep the elbows in close to the body.

Figure 5-15

### Push-ups

*Purpose.* Arm and shoulder strength.

*Procedure.* Assume a straight-arm support position with the weight on the toes and the hands. Lower the body until the chest touches the floor (Fig. 5-16). Return to the starting position.

*Precaution.* Keep the body in a straight line by contracting the trunk and hip muscles. Do not arch the back. Keep the elbows in close to the body.

Figure 5-16

### Trunk Lifts

*Purpose.* Upper-back strength.

*Procedure.* In a prone position, with the arms extended, clasp the hands together behind the lower back. Beginning with the head, lift the upper body off the floor as high as possible (Fig. 5-17). Hold the position four counts and return to the starting position.

*Precaution.* Keep the feet on the floor. Do not rotate or jerk.

Figure 5-17

### Leg Lifts

*Purpose.* Hip strength.

*Procedure.* From a prone position, tighten the muscles in the hip area and while keeping the hip bone on the floor, lift the right leg as high as possible (Fig. 5-18). Hold this position four counts and return to the starting position. Repeat the exercise with the left leg.

*Precaution.* Keep the leg straight. Do not lift the hip off the floor.

*Note.* An alternate position for this exercise is to bend the leg at the knee and keep the toes pointed upward.

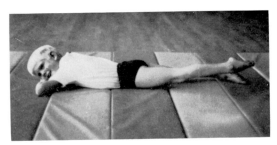

Figure 5-18

### Arm Lifts

*Purpose.* Shoulder strength.

*Procedure.* From a prone position with the arms extended outward at shoulder level, pinch the shoulder blades together and lift the arms upward as high as possible (Fig. 5-19). Hold this position four counts and return to the starting position. Second progression: Bend the arms at the elbow and perform the exercise in the same manner (Fig. 5-20). Third progression: Place the arms outstretched in midposition between the shoulders and the head (Fig. 5-21). Perform the exercise in the same manner. Fourth progression: Place the arms directly over the head and perform the exercise in the same manner (Fig. 5-22). Each position is a progression of the original exercise and should not be attempted until ten repetitions of the previous progression can be done.

*Precaution.* Pull the shoulder blades together before lifting the arms. Keep the head and trunk on the floor. Maintain the original arm position throughout the exercise.

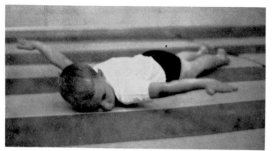

Figure 5-19

Figure 5-20

Figure 5-21

Figure 5-22

### Partial Knee Bends

*Purpose.* Leg strength.

*Procedure.* From a standing position with the hands on the hips, raise to the toes on count one (Fig. 5-23). On count two bend the knees to a semisquat position (Fig. 5-24). On count three return to the straight-leg position with the weight still on the toes. On count four return to a flat-foot poistion.

*Precaution.* Do not bounce into a full squat position. Keep the trunk straight.

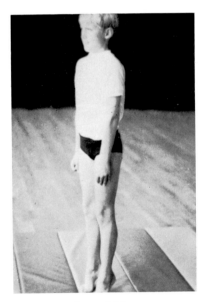

Figure 5-23

Figure 5-24

### Arm Patterns

*Purpose.* Coordination and shoulder strength.

*Procedure.* Assume a standing position with the arms at the sides of the body. Move the hands up over the head and clap them (Fig. 5-25). Return the arms to the side with a slap on the side of the thighs (Fig. 5-26). Clap the hands in front, shoulder high (Fig. 5-27). Clap the hands behind the back (Fig. 5-28). Repeat the exercise ten times. Increase five repetitions each exercise period until twenty-five is reached.

*Precaution.* Keep the shoulders and back straight.

Figure 5-25

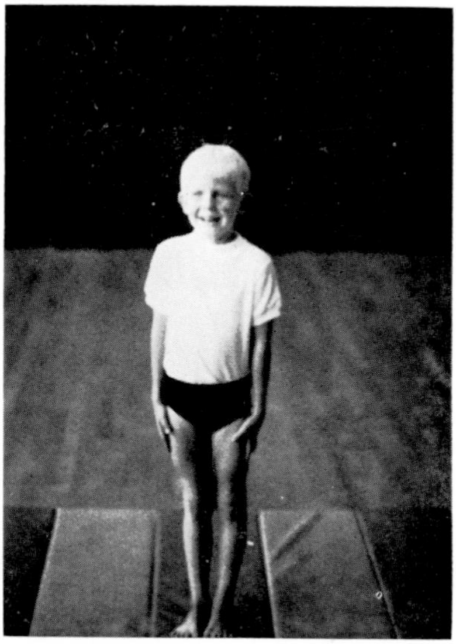

Figure 5-26

Figure 5-27

Figure 5-28

### Foot Patterns

*Purpose.* Coordination and leg strength.

*Procedure.* Stand in an erect position with the feet together. On count one, jump to a side-stride position with the feet shoulder-width apart (Fig. 5-29). Return to the starting position on count two. On count three, jump to a forward-stride position with one foot forward and the other foot backward (Fig. 5-30). Return to the starting position on count four. After the movement pattern is learned, alternate the right and left foot in the forward position of the forward stride. Repeat the exercise ten times. Increase five repetitions each exercise period until twenty-five is reached.

*Precaution.* Land lightly on the balls of the feet with the knees slightly bent.

Figure 5-29                     Figure 5-30

### Jumping Jacks

*Purpose.* Cardiovascular endurance and general body conditioning.

*Procedure.* From a standing position, jump to a side-stride position and simultaneously clap the hands together over the head. Jump and return to the starting position. Repeat the exercise ten times. Increase five repetitions each exercise period until fifty is reached.

*Precaution.* Perform the exercise smoothly.

## Running

*Purpose.* General body conditioning and endurance.

*Procedure.* Running may be done in various forms. Each form requires a little different muscle action and energy output. Jogging is a moderate run used for endurance conditioning. Running in place using a high knee action is good cardiovascular conditioning and will help slenderize the abdominal area (Fig. 5-31). Dashes require a complete output in a short time and are excellent for general body conditioning and leg strength. Running activities should be a basic part of each day's conditioning program and it may be done in many different ways: relays, races, games, circuit training, or as a jogging club program.

*Precaution.* In each form of running, care should be taken to land on the balls of the feet with a slight knee bend to absorb the force of the movement and prevent injury to the legs and back.

Figure 5-31

### Squat Thrusts

*Purpose.* General body conditioning, coordination, and agility.

*Procedure.* Start from a standing position with the arm at the side. Move through the partial knee-bend position to a front-lean position with the trunk bent and the weight on the hands and feet. Extend the legs to a straight body-lean position (Fig. 5-32). Return to the hand and foot support position and subsequently to a strength standing position.

*Precaution.* Go through the complete range of motion in each position. Do not bounce to a full-squat position.

Figure 5-32

## Apparatus Activities

### Passive Hang

*Purpose.* Arm, shoulder, and head flexibility and strength.

*Procedure.* Hang by the hands from a horizontal bar. Stretch to become as long as possible (Fig. 5-33). Hold this position five seconds.

*Precaution.* Grip firmly.

### Active Hang

*Purpose.* Arm, shoulder, and hand flexibility and strength.

*Procedure.* Hang by the hands from a horizontal bar and twist, turn, and kick (Fig. 5-34).

*Precaution.* Grip firmly. Dismount lightly with the knees slightly bent.

Figure 5-33                    Figure 5-34

### Chin-up

*Purpose.* Arm, shoulder, and hand strength.

*Procedure.* Grip the horizontal bar with the palms toward the performer. From a stationary hanging position, pull to a position with the chin on top of the bar (Fig. 5-35). Return to a straight hanging position. Note: If the child is unable to begin this exercise, a modified chin-up may be done from a backward leaning position with the bar approximately shoulder high and the feet partially supporting the body weight.

*Precaution.* Grip firmly.

### Pull-up

*Purpose.* Arm, shoulder, and hand strength.

*Procedure.* Grip the horizontal bar with the palms turned away from the performer. From a stationary position, pull to a position with the chin on top of the bar (Fig. 5-36). Return to a straight hanging position. Note: A modified pull-up may be done in the same manner described for the modified chin-up.

*Precaution.* Grip firmly.

Figure 5-35                    Figure 5-36

### Knee Tuck

*Purpose.* Abdominal strength.

*Procedure.* While hanging by the hands from a horizontal bar, lift the knees to the chest (Fig. 5-37). Hold this position for five seconds and return to the starting position.

*Precaution.* Do not swing the knees up.

Figure 5-37

## L-Hang

*Purpose.* Abdominal strength.

*Procedure.* While hanging by the hands from a horizontal bar, lift the legs to a horizontal position, parallel to the floor (Fig. 5-38). Hold the position for five seconds and return to a straight hanging position.

*Precaution.* Keep the legs straight.

Figure 5-38

## Bench Steps

*Purpose.* Leg strength, endurance, and coordination.

*Procedure.* Stand in an erect position facing a bench approximately eighteen inches high. Step onto the bench with the right foot, bring the left foot onto the bench, and come to an erect standing position with the knees straight. Step down to the floor with the right foot, bring the left foot to the floor, and assume the starting position for the next repetition. Repeat the exercise ten times with the right foot leading and ten times with the left foot leading. For endurance, do additional repetitions by adding sets of ten.

*Precaution.* Come to a complete erect position on the bench with the knees straight. Do the exercise to a four-count rhythmical pattern.

The American Association for Health, Physical Education, and Recreation has sponsored many programs for the handicapped student. The Project on Recreation and Fitness for the Mentally Retarded is one such program which it has sponsored in cooporation with the Joseph P. Kennedy Jr. Foundation. As a part of this program, the AAHPER has extended its fitness program to include a test of physical fitness especially adapted for mentally retarded boys and girls.

Mentally retarded children have the same need for physical development and recreation that normal children do. However, standards of performance used for normal children are not appropriate for most mentally retarded children. The AAHPER *Special Fitness Test Manual*\* has adapted the tests recommended for normal children to the ability of the mentally retarded. The tests may be used as a means of assessing the physical fitness level, as a diagnosis of strength and weakness, and as an incentive for the mentally retarded child to improve his level of fitness and motor performance. The manual also provides national norms with which to compare the level of performance and measure the progress of each child. An awards system is also contained in the test manual. Emblems may be obtained for the retarded boys and girls who meet specific levels of physical fitness.

------

\*The AAHPER *Special Fitness Test Manual for the Mentally Retarded* may be obtained by contacting the NEA Publications-Sales, 1201 Sixteenth St., N.W., Washington, D.C. 20036.

## Circuit Training

Circuit training is an approach to the exercise program that can provide a creative experience to aid the student as he participates. Circuit training consists of a series of stations placed throughout the gymnasium or exercise area with specific exercises outlined for each station. The directions of the circuit may be to do the required exercise at each station and to complete the entire circuit in the shortest amount of time possible. The objective of this type of circuit is to develop cardiovascular endurance, or as it is commonly called, physical fitness. The directions of another circuit may be to follow instructions at each station and to do the exercises as directed with no emphasis placed upon time for completing the circuit. The objective of this type of circuit would be the strengthening of specific muscle groups, coordination, or a combination, that could also include physical fitness development.

The circuit-training approach should be used only after the children are thoroughly familiar with the exercises and have been carefully instructed concerning what to do. Small groups of children can function well on a circuit course if a leader is present to read the directions and to help each child perform the required exercises. Retarded children may need encouragement in the form of cheering and clapping in order to score well if the time it takes to do the circuit is being recorded. Once the circuit course is set and the children are in the process of learning the sequence of the exercises, care should be taken not to change the order of the stations or the sequence of the prescribed exercises at each station. One of the associated learnings of the circuit-training experience is that of improving the ability of the child to remember directions and to follow instructions. The directions for each station can be printed on cards of different colors, and reference can be made to specific exercise groups by referring to the color of the cards. The children will soon make the station, exercise, and color association.

The entire circuit should not be presented at once. Each station should be presented to and learned by the children before advancing on the next station. The entire sequence will be learn-

ed and at that point the circuit-training experience will start to
have meaning and the child will benefit from the experience.

Examples of circuit-training stations with exercises that place
emphasis upon physical fitness are listed below:

*Station 1.* Twenty-five jumping jacks. Run to next station.

*Station 2.* Ten bent-leg sit-ups. Roll to the next station.

*Station 3.* Five full push-ups. Run to the next station.

*Station 4.* Crawl under five chairs. Run to the next station.

*Station 5.* Run in place for thirty counts. Count one each
time each foot touches the floor. Run backwards to the next
station.

*Station 6.* Do stride-together-stride-together down a pattern.
Run to end of course.

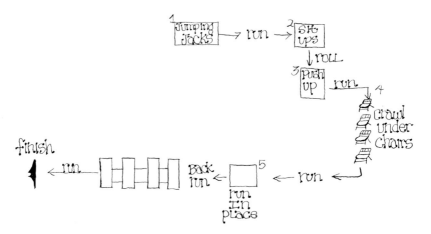

Examples of circuit-training station exercises with emphasis
upon strengthening specific muscle groups and physical fitness are
as follows:

*Station 1.* Abdominal strength.

    1. Ten bent-leg sit-ups.

    2. Ten hand and knee cat contractions.

    3. Ten diagonal sit-ups, five to each side.

*Station 2.* Shoulder strength.

    1. Isometric hand presses, three positions (Figs. 5-39, 5-40,
      5-41).

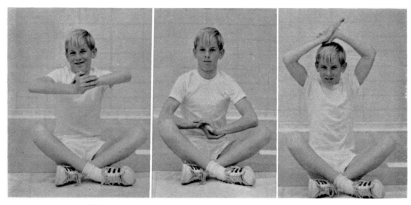

Figure 5-39          Figure 5-40          Figure 5-41

    2. Five arm raises, three positions.

    3. Three bent-leg push-ups.

*Station 3.* Leg and hip strength and slenderizing.

    1. Five leg raises from front lying position.

    2. Five side leg lifts, five on each side (Fig. 5-42).

    3. Hip walk, ten counts forward and ten counts backward (Fig. 5-43).

*Station 4.* Back strength.

    1. Upper-body raises, five straight.

    2. Upper-body raises, five to each side.

Figure 5-42

Figure 5-43

*Station 5.* Foot strength.
    1. Towel gathering (Fig. 5-44).
    2. Marble pick-up (Fig. 5-45).

Figure 5-44                Figure 5-45

*Station 6.* Endurance.
    1. Two-minute run around the room as fast as possible.

The students can function as one group with everyone doing the exercises together, or the class can be put into squads with each squad starting at different stations and going through the entire circuit.

# Chapter 6

# STUNTS AND TUMBLING

Two of the recognized objectives of physical education are the development of physical fitness and the development of performance skill. The activities included in this chapter all require strength, flexibility, endurance, and coordination and thus contribute to the physical well-being of the individual child performer. Each stunt has form and function peculiar to it, and the development of this skill is satisfying and fun for the child.

The retarded child has missed the experiences of the normal child of rough-and tumble play on the living-room carpet and of rolls and cartwheels on the front lawn on a summer evening. Protected as he is, the retarded child is often not physically strong enough to join safely in this activity with the normal children; consequently he cannot participate in group activity and has not been included in normal neighborhood activities.

Emphasis in the stunts and tumbling activities unit should be on exploring, being animals, solving problems, experimenting, and learning. The child should be assisted when he needs it; he should be encouraged to perform his best each time. A child will need courage to perform even the most simple stunt because his experience in performing has been limited. He can develop this courage, and this learning can carry over into his other daily experiences. His feelings of *self* are improved with the experience in activities that challenge his total body.

## Teaching Suggestions

Listed below are some suggestions for the teacher of stunts and tumbling:

1. The group for each teacher should be small—five or six children for each leader is the maximum at the beginning of the activity. As the experience of the group increases, the size of the group can be enlarged.

2. Mats should be available and should always be used.

3. As each child performs he should be praised and receive positive reinforcement.

4. The pace of the activities should be kept moving. Children waiting too long for a turn will become bored and require discipline, which can change the entire feeling about the activity.

5. The teacher should know the activity. The inexperienced teacher does not know or understand the fears a child has about a stunt or the hazards involved in the activities.

6. The teacher should progress slowly and increase the skill difficulty gradually. When a child can perform a stunt efficiently, move on to another, more difficult and demanding stunt.

7. The teacher should be the spotter for each child until he can perform efficiently, and then the child should be encouraged to perform without a spotter but should always perform.

8. Each lesson should be started with a review of the previous lesson. This review will set the mood for the lesson and will help the student recall what was done.

9. Each child should be called by name and signals or commands should be used. Example: "Tommy, be ready, tuck your chin and roll."

10. When there is more than one teacher for the group, each should plan to use the same lesson outline for each daily lesson, but should be free to change the lesson for her own group on any particular day.

11. Each teacher should have the same group of children each day. A child develops a relationship for performance with a teacher. The teacher should recognize the amount of effort needed for a single-stunt performance for the first time.

12. Tumbling stunts should not be used for relay races. Accidents can happen any time in a tumbling program and racing is especially hazardous because it often causes the performer to forget cautions.

The following list and description of activities is placed as nearly as possible in order of progression difficulty. Each stunt requires balance, strength, flexibility, timing, agility, and coordination.

### Heel Click

*Starting Position.* Stand with the feet twelve inches apart.

*Action.* Jump into the air and click the heels together (Fig. 6-1) and land with the feet apart.

### Balance

*Starting Position.* Stand with the hands on the hips.

*Action.* Close the eyes, raise one foot, and balance as long as possible (Fig. 6-2) .

Figure 6-1                    Figure 6-2

### Tightrope Walking

*Starting Position.* Stand with both feet on a line.

*Action.* Walk down the line without stepping off the line.

### Lame Dog

*Starting Position.* Weight on the hands and on one leg. Keep the other leg bent and off the mat. (See Fig. 6-3.)

*Action.* Walk forward.

Figure 6-3

### Wicket Walk

*Starting Position.* Stand, bend over, and take hold of each ankle.

*Action.* Walk, keeping the knees as straight as possible (Fig. 6-4).

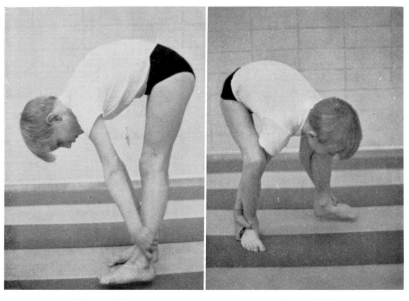

Figure 6-4                              Figure 6-5

### Cricket Walk

*Starting Position.* Assume the squat position, put the hands between the knees and around behind the ankles, and take hold of the top of the feet.

*Action.* Walk forward (Fig. 6-5).

### Tuck Jump

*Starting Position.* Assume the squat position and hold both knees together with both arms.

*Action.* Jump forward; do not let go of the knees (Fig. 6-6).

Figure 6-6

### Submarine

*Starting Position.* Lie on the back, placing the hands on bent knees.

*Action.* Raise the head and push the body along the floor by pushing with the feet and sliding the body backward (Fig. 6-7).

### Side Roll

*Starting Position.* Lie on the back, bend the knees to the chest, bend elbows, and put hands on the shoulders.

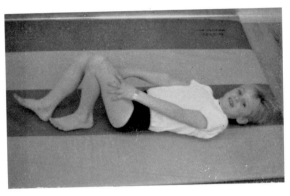

Figure 6-7

*Action.* Roll to either side and come to a position on hands and knees (Fig. 6-8).

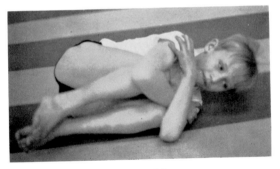

Figure 6-8

### Bear Walk
*Starting Position.* Assume front-lean position with arms and legs straight.
*Action.* Lift the right leg and the right arm and move forward, keeping arms and legs straight. Repeat with left side (Fig. 6-9).

### Seal Walk
*Starting Position.* Support body with weight on the hands, and legs extended behind.

Figure 6-9

*Action.* Walk on the hands and drag the feet (Fig. 6-10).

Figure 6-10

### Crab Walk

*Starting Position.* Sit with hands on the floor behind the hips and raise the body.

*Action.* Walk on the hands and feet, keeping the body straight (Fig. 6-11).

### Top Spin

*Starting Position.* Stand with the feet apart.

*Action.* Jump, turn, and land facing one-quarter turn to the

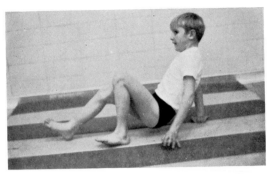

Figure 6-11

right; jump, turn, and land facing one-half turn to the right; jump, turn, and land facing three-quarter turn to the right; jump, turn and land making one full turn to right. Repeat the entire sequence to the left. (Figs. 6-12 and 6-13).

Figure 6-12                     Figure 6-13

## V-Sit

*Starting Position.* Assume long sitting position with the hands on the mat behind the body.

*Action.* Lean the upper body back and raise both feet. Keep legs straight and hold for five seconds (Fig. 6-14).

Figure 6-14

## Timber

*Starting Position.* Kneel with the body straight and the arms extended at a 45-degree angle.

*Action.* Fall forward and catch the body with the arms just as the mat is reached (Fig. 6-15).

Figure 6-15

## Rabbit Kick

*Starting Position.* Assume a squat position with the knees together, the arms extended forward, and the head up.

*Action.* Dive forward onto the hands, keeping the knees bent and the feet close to the hips. Look at the mat. (Fig. 6-16.) Return to starting position.

Figure 6-16

### Mule Kick

*Starting Position.* Stand at the edge of a mat with the hands extended overhead.

*Action.* Place the hands on the mat and kick the legs above the hips. Look at the mat. (Fig. 6-17.) Return to starting position.

Figure 6-17

### Frog Stand

*Starting Position.* Kneeling, place the hands on a mat even with the knees. Place the head on the mat in front of the hands to form a triangle.

*Action.* Raise the hips and place the knees one at a time on the elbows (Fig. 6-18). Hold for three seconds. Return to starting position.

Figure 6-18

## Partner Stunts and Easy Combatives

### Bouncing Ball

*Starting Position.* One person (the ball) squats and holds the knees with the arms. The partner (bouncer) stands behind with his hands on the "ball's" upper back.

*Action.* The bouncer pushes the ball and makes it bounce (Fig. 6-19). The ball responds to the pressure exerted.

### Wring the Dishrag

*Starting Position.* Partners face each other and join hands.

*Action.* The arms are raised as the partners turn away from each other under the raised arms (Fig. 6-20). They return to face each other as the opposite arms are raised.

Figure 6-19                    Figure 6-20

### Sawing Wood

*Starting Position.* Partners face each other each with one foot forward and take hold of hands.

*Action.* Push opposite arms back and forward, pretending to saw wood (Fig. 6-21).

### Chinese Get-up

*Starting Position.* Partners of equal size stand back to back with elbows hooked.

*Action.* By pushing against each others' back, lower to a sitting position (Fig. 6-22) and then rise to a standing position.

### Seesaw

*Starting Position.* Partners face each other and join hands. One partner stands and the other squats.

*Action.* Partners move at the same time and each finishes in the opposite position (Fig. 6-23). Repeat at a faster rate of speed.

Figure 6-21                    Figure 6-22

Figure 6-23

## Twister

*Starting Position.* Partners stand back to back with legs apart and with the left hand on the left knee. Reach through the legs with the right hand and grasp partner's right hand (Fig. 6-24).

*Action.* Keeping hands gripped, one child swings his right leg over the partner's back. Then the partner swings his right leg over the clasped hands (Fig. 6-25). They are now facing each other. One child swings his left leg over clasped hands, the other partner swings his left leg over his partner's back. They are now in starting position.

Figure 6-24                    Figure 6-25

### Siamese Twin Walk

*Starting Position.* Stand back to back with the elbows hooked together.

*Action.* Walk together; one walks forward and the other backward (Fig. 6-26).

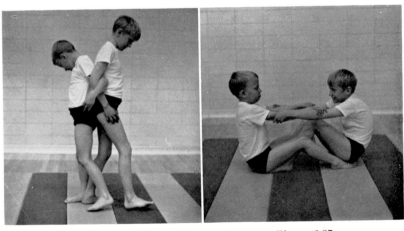

Figure 6-26                    Figure 6-27

### Rocker

*Starting Position.* Partners sit facing each other; each one sits on the other's feet. The legs are bent. Each grasps the other's arms at the elbow (Fig. 6-27).

*Action.* One partner leans back and the other rises from the mat to a standing position. Reverse action and continue rocking.

### Swim

*Starting Position.* One partner is sitting with the legs bent and the hands on the floor behind the hips. The other partner backs onto the sitting partner, locks his ankles behind the sitting partner, and arches his back.

*Action.* Sitting partner scoots along the floor, supporting himself with his hands, lifting the hips, and bending and extending the legs. Partner on top swims the breast stroke and together they move along floor (Fig. 6-28). (Breast stroke: Extend arms to side, tuck arms under body, and extend forward.)

Figure 6-28

### Push the Donkey

*Starting Position.* Partners stand one behind the other, both facing the same direction.

*Action.* The person behind attempts to push the other over a line. The partner in front resists by pushing backward (Fig. 6-29).

Figure 6-29

### Crab Fight

*Starting Position.* Assume crab-walk poistion side by side.

*Action.* On the signal, each tries to push the other off balance (Fig. 6-30).

Figure 6-30

### Back to Back

*Starting Position.* Partners sit down back to back.

*Action.* Using the hands and the feet, each tries to push the partner without lifting his own seat from the floor (Fig. 6-31). Keep the head down.

Figure 6-31

## Tumbling Skills

The importance of correct spotting during each of the activities included in this tumbling series cannot be overstressed. It is the responsibility of the teacher to insure safe participation throughout the entire unit of instruction. Spotting correctly is one of the ways to keep tumbling safe and fun.

### Spotting Techniques for the Forward Roll

*Starting Position.* Kneel at the side of the performer.

*Action.* Place one hand at the base of performer's neck, the other hand at his hips. Give support to the head, keeping it tucked, and help direct the roll with the hand at the hips (Fig. 6-32).

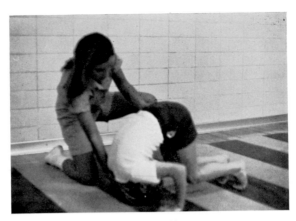

Figure 6-32

### Forward Roll Sequence

*Starting Position 1.* Kneel on the mat, put hands on the mat in front of the knees, and put head on mat between hands. Keep the chin tucked close to chest (Fig. 6-33).

*Action.* Lift hips, look between the legs, *roll* to the back of the shoulders, push with feet and hands, and roll over, supporting the weight with the hands. End roll with feet together and knees close to the chest.

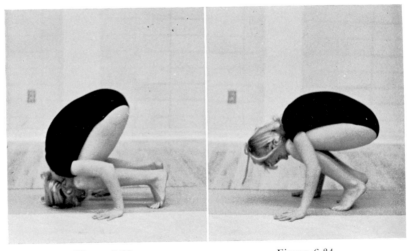

Figure 6-33                        Figure 6-34

| Figure 6-35 | Figure 6-36 |

*Starting Position 2.* Squat on the mat and put hands on the mat in front of the knees (Fig. 6-34).

*Action.* Keep the chin tucked, brush the head lightly on the mat as the hips are lifted and the feet push. Roll over, supporting the weight with the hands (Fig. 6-35), and land on upper back. End the roll with feet together and knees close to the chest.

*Starting Position 3.* Squat on the mat with the arms extended.

*Action.* Rock forward, place the hands, brush the head lightly on the mat, and push with the feet and roll, supporting the weight with the hands. Land gently on upper back. End roll with the feet together and knees close to chest. Repeat action but end roll by continuing forward and finish in a squat position.

*Starting Position 4.* Stand on the mat. Bend the knees; extend arms downward.

*Action.* Reach forward and downward, place the hands on the mat (Fig. 6-36), and brush the head lightly on the mat, keeping the chin tucked. Push with the feet and roll over. End roll in a squatting position.

*Starting Position 5.* Stand with arms at the sides.

*Action.* Swing the arms forward and place the hands on the mat. At same time tuck the head, brush lightly on the mat, lift the hips, and complete the roll. End roll by standing up.

*Do not include dive rolls over other children when working with mentally retarded children. The chance for serious injury is very great.*

### Spotting Techniques for the Back Roll

*Starting Position.* Stand at side of the tumble and in the line of direction of the roll. Place hands at the hip joint.

*Action.* As the tumbler starts the roll, lift (do not *push*) the tumbler at the hips (Fig. 6-37).

Figure 6-37

### Back Roll Sequence

*Starting Position 1.* Sit with the knees bent and hands on the knees (Fig. 6-38).

*Action.* Roll back (Fig. 6-39) until the feet touch the mat behind the head. Return to a sitting position.

*Starting Position 2.* Sit with the knees bent, hands on the knees, and head down close to knees (Fig. 6-40).

*Action.* Rock forward and roll back; release the hands and place them on the mat with the thumbs next to the ears and push to complete the roll. Keep the chin tucked. End in a kneeling position. Repeat action but end in a squatting position.

*Starting Position 3*. Squat with the head close to the knees and the arms around the knees (Fig. 6-41).

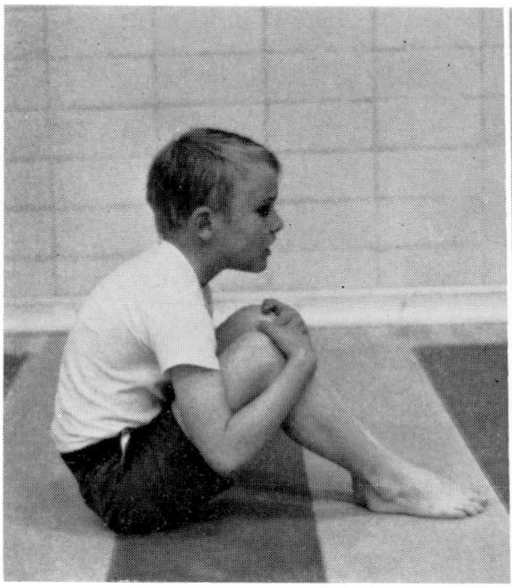

Figure 6-38

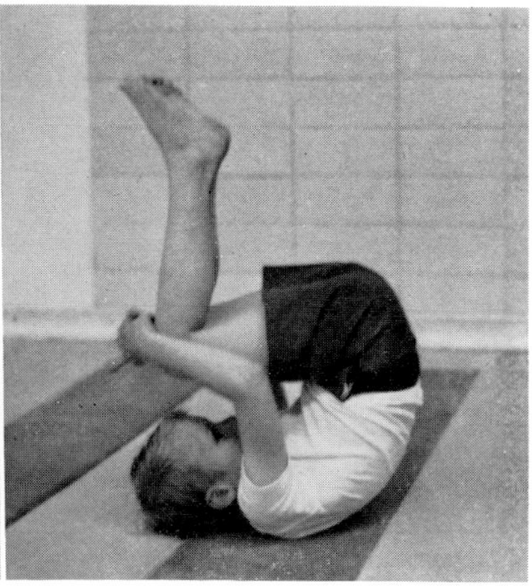

Figure 6-39

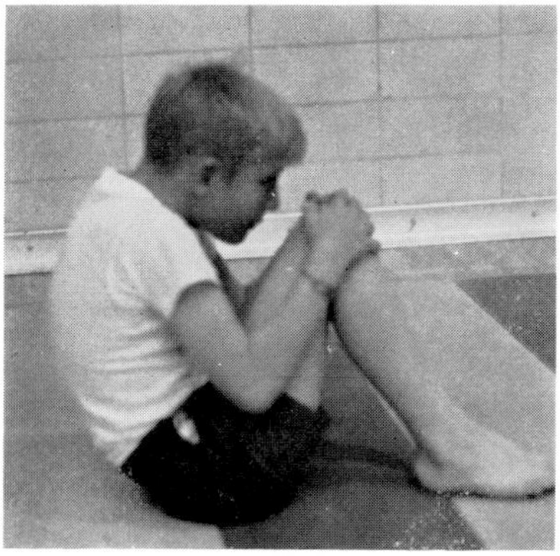

Figure 6-40

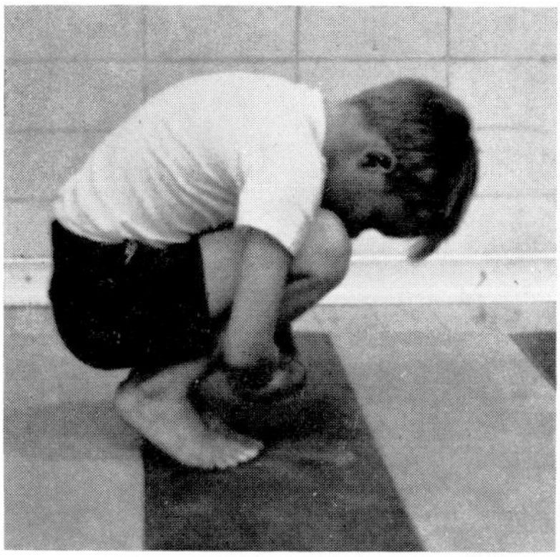

Figure 6-41

*Action*. Rock forward; roll back, push with the hands placed on mat by the ears (Fig. 6-42). Roll over and finish in a squatting position.

*Starting Position 4*. Stand.

*Action*. Drop to a squat and complete roll as in preceding action.

Figure 6-42

*Starting Position 5.* Assume stride-standing position, the hands between the knees (Fig. 6-43).

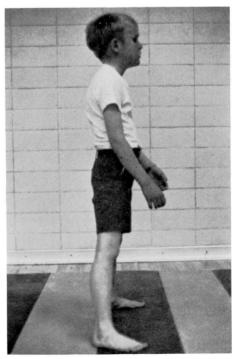

Figure 6-43

*Action.* Sit down, catching the body with the hands. Change the hands onto the mat even with the ears and complete roll. Finish in a stride-standing position.

### Spotting Techniques for the Cartwheel

*Starting Position.* Spotter stands behind the tumbler and places his hands on the tumbler's waist, using a cross-arm grip (Fig. 6-44).

*Action.* As the cartwheel is performed, the arms uncross and are parallel at the end of the stunt. Move with cartwheel and give support throughout.

Figure 6-44

### Cartwheel Sequence

*Starting Position 1.* Each child draws a circle on the floor with chalk. Stand sideways to the circle. Bend down to put nearest hand in the circle. Turn body to put other hand in the circle (Fig. 6-45).

*Action.* Keep both hands in the circle. Swing legs over the circle (Fig. 6-46) and come to a standing position.

Figure 6-45

Figure 6-46

*Starting Position 2.* Same as #1; swing the legs up over the hips (Fig. 6-47).

Figure 6-47

*Starting Position 3.* Tumbler stands close to a rope held about knee height by two other children.

*Action.* Reach over the rope with the arms and kick legs over one at a time (Fig. 6-48).

Figure 6-48

*Starting Position 4.* Stand with body bent and arms extended toward mat.

*Action.* Thrust arms to the mat one after the other. Swing up outer leg as other leg pushes off (Fig. 6-49) and land on leading leg.

*Starting Position 5.* Stand facing the mat, arms back extended overhead.

*Action.* Kick one leg forward, hop, and step forward. Count 1: Place the same hand on the mat to the side of the foot. Count 2: Place the other hand on the mat in a line on the mat. Kick both legs up until the hips are over the head. Count 3: Place one leg on the mat in the straight line. Count 4: Place the other leg on the mat.

Figure 6-49

## Spotting Techniques for Head Stand

*Starting Position.* Place one hand at the base of the tumbler's neck and give pressure. Place the other hand at the tumbler's hips to give support and direction (Fig. 6-50).

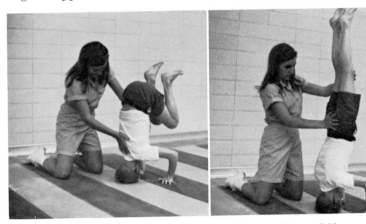

Figure 6-50                    Figure 6-51

*Action.* As the tumbler lifts his hips, give support at the base of the neck. Keep his body straight and his weight equally distributed between his hands and his head. (Fig. 6-51). *Do not hold the tumbler at the ankles.*

### Head Stand Sequence

*Starting Position 1.* Review frog stand (p. 97). Take starting position for frog stand; slowly extend the legs overhead and balance. Return to starting position.

*Starting Position 2.* Kneel with the hands shoulder-width apart in line with the knees; place the head with hairline on the mat, *not the top of the head.* Hands and head are in a triangle. Caution: Do not balance on top of the head.

*Action.* Lift the hips above the shoulders, and push the feet upward until the legs are straight and back is slightly arched.

*Starting Position 3.* Same as #2.

*Action.* Push off the mat with toes of both feet, flex the knees, and raise the body to a half-way position. Extend both legs.

# Chapter 7

# APPARATUS ACTIVITIES

## TRAMPOLINE

$A$ section on skills for the trampoline has been included in this text because trampoline equipment is often available for special education classroom units. Equipment is often donated to the school system and the special education unit, being the smallest classroom unit in the school, has use of this equipment.

The teacher of an instructional unit on the trampoline must understand the hazards involved with this very popular piece of apparatus. Children can be seriously injured during activity on the trampoline.

Included in this section are the very basic skills from which simple routines can be created. It is recommened that if there is a need for more complex skills the teacher should go to the gymnastic coach for assistance and advanced training.

### Teaching Suggestions for the Trampoline

The following are some suggestions for the teacher of trampoline skills:

1. Make each turn for each child short. If the waiting time is too long the value of using the trampoline is lost.

2. Give each child a specific number of jumps or stunts to do.

3. Remind each child at each turn what he is to perform.

4. Keep track of the performing order of the group.

5. Remind the child to jump in the center of the mat.

6. Get on the mat with a child if that particular child needs your help.

7. Have a child repeat verbally what he is to do before he performs the sequence.

8. *Never leave the trampoline open and unattended by a trained leader.*

114

## Trampoline Skills

### *Easy Bounce*

Stand in the center of the mat, bend knees, and jump, pushing down with toes. Swing arms over head (Fig. 7-1). Land with feet apart. Jump five times and get off.

### *Half-Pirouette*

Stand in the center of the mat; jump two times. Swing one arm over head and turn toward that arm (Fig. 7-2). Make a half-turn. Jump two times and half-pirouette again.

Figure 7-1                         Figure 7-2

### *Knee Drop*

Stand in the center of the mat; drop to the knees with the feet extended behind, arms extended to the side (Fig. 7-3). Keep the knees on the center of the mat. Push into the mat with the legs and return to standing position. Repeat: feet, knees, feet, knees, feet.

Figure 7-3

Figure 7-4

### Hand and Knee Drop

Stand in the center of the mat; drop to the knees and the hands (Fig. 7-4). Hit mat with the knees and with the hands at the same time. Keep the center of the body at the center of the mat. Push into the mat and place the feet at the center of the mat. Repeat: drop, jump, drop, jump.

### Seat Drop

Stand in center of the mat. Push into mat and jump slightly. Extend both legs and sit in center of the mat with hands on mat even with the hips. Push into the mat and jump in the center of the mat (Fig. 7-5). Repeat: drop, jump, drop, jump.

### Seat Drop and Half-Twist to Stand

Stand in the center of the mat facing one end of the mat. Perform a seat drop. Push into mat and turn and jump facing opposite end of mat (Fig. 7-6). Repeat: seat drop, turn, jump, seat drop, turn, jump.

### Swivel Hip

Stand in the center of the mat facing one end of mat. Perform a set drop, push into mat, and swing both arms over head. Twist body and perform another seat drop facing opposite ends of mat.

Figure 7-5           Figure 7-6

A trampoline routine can consist of ten contacts with the mat. Simple routines can be made up by the teacher and by the children from the above list of beginning stunts. A simple routine might be seat drop (1) to a stand (2), half-pirouette (3), half-pirouette (4), hand and knee drop (5) to a stand (6), seat drop and turn (7), half-piroutte (8), deep jump with legs extended (9), jump (10).

## BALANCE BEAM

Every child seems naturally attracted to the walking of a rail, a fence, or a beam. This skill requires balance, coordination, and timing. A child with motor problems, whether he be retarded or not, will not enjoy this experience freely. He will need to be taught, assisted, and encouraged to perform. Fear enters a great deal into the performance of the skill. The overcoming of this fear can help the child to be more able to solve other problems that he may meet during his daily activities.

The specific values derived from working on the balance beam are those inherent in perceptual-motor experiences. By walking the beam a child learns to balance while standing motionless. He can change his balance by weighting one side or the other. He can test his balance by changing his level on the beam. There are some tests available that make use of the balance beam in testing a child's ability to maintain balance, his laterality, and his perceptual skills in general.

### Prebalance Beam Skills

The prebalance beam skill progression is as follows:

1. Practice walking first on the floor.
2. Practice walking on a line on the floor.
3. Practice walking on a board (2 × 4) that is laying flat on the floor.
4. Practice walking on a low beam.
5. Practice walking on an intermediate beam about two feet from the floor.
6. Practice walking finally on a high beam five feet from the floor.

### Balance Beam Skills

When performing all the skills described below, it is important to remember that good posture is to be maintained throughout the stunt.

1. *Walking Forward.* The arms are raised to the side, the head is up, and the body is erect. The eyes should be watching for the end of the beam. (Do not watch the feet.) Place one foot in front of the other, feel the beam, and walk down the beam (Fig. 7-7).

2. *Giant Steps.* Observe erect posture with the arms raised. Take big steps and progress down the beam (Fig. 7-8).

3. *Big Step-Little Step.* Take one big step and one little step and progress down the beam.

4. *Sideward Steps.* Stand on the beam with the side facing the end of the beam, hands to the side, and the body erect. Step to the side with the leading foot and bring the other foot up to it. Repeat to the end of the beam (Fig. 7-9).

Figure 7-7                    Figure 7-8

5. *Side Crossover.* Side position as in #4. Cross the nonleading foot over in front of the lead foot, step to the side, and progress to the end of the beam (Fig. 7-10) .

Figure 7-9                    Figure 7-10

6. *Backward Walk.* Stand on the beam, take a step backward, place one foot directly behind the other, feel the beam, and progress to the end of the beam (Fig. 7-11).

Figure 7-11                    Figure 7-12

7. *Pivot.* Stand on the beam at the center facing one end of the beam. The feet are one step apart. Rise onto the balls of both feet, turn slowly, face the opposite direction, and carefully put the heels down on the beam. Arms can extend sideways to assist in the lift and turn (Fig. 7-12).

8. *Walk-Pivot-Return.* Walk to the center of the beam, pivot, and walk to the starting end of the beam.

9. *Walk-Pivot-Continue.* Walk to the center of the beam, pivot, and walk backward to the end of the beam.

10. *Scale Balance.* Stand on the beam, balance on one leg, raise the other leg straight backward, and extend both arms forward. The body is in as horizontal a position as possible (Fig. 7-13).

Figure 7-13

11. *Arabesque.* Stand on the beam on one leg. The other leg is bent at the knee and the knee is raised. The arms raise overhead and the body is erect (Fig. 7-14).

Figure 7-14

12. *Knee Scale.* Kneel on the beam. The weight is supported on one knee and foreleg, and on both hands. The other leg is extended backward and the head is up (Fig. 7-15).

Figure 7-15

13. *Mounting the High or Intermediate Beam.* Sit sidesaddle on the beam. Swing one leg over the beam (Fig. 7-16). Swing both legs forward and backward and place the feet on the beam behind (Fig. 7-17). With the hands and feet on the beam, push into a standing position.

14. *Dismounting.* Place one hand on the beam for support (Fig. 7-18). Jump off.

15. *Obstacle Course.* Place beams of different heights end to end to make a trail or route to follow. The children can just walk all of the beams, or, as they become more skilled, stunts can be performed as the trail is practiced.

16. *Simple Routine.* Mount, take three steps, pivot, arabesque, pivot, knee scale, stand, dismount.

### Balance Beam Jumping Skills

There are many stunts to be performed on the balance beam. The objective of the chapter is to present a sequential progression of skills to provide the teacher in special education with enough materials to include the balance beam in her program of physical

Figure 7-16          Figure 7-17          Figure 7-18

education. The following is a list of jumping skills to be done on the low beam requiring balance skill as well as jumping skill.

1. Stand on the beam, jump off the beam, and jump back onto the beam. Progress to the end of the beam.

2. Stand on the beam, jump off the beam with both feet on the right side of the beam, and jump back onto the beam. Progress to the end of the beam.

3. Stand on the beam, jump off the beam with both feet on the left side of the beam, and jump back onto the beam. Progress to the end of the beam.

4. Stand on the floor beside the beam. Jump onto the beam and jump off the beam landing on the floor at the other side of the beam. Continue to the end of the beam.

5. Stand on the floor at the side of the beam. Jump over the beam to the other side of the beam. Continue jumping over the beam as you progress to the end.

Additional skills and stunts for the balance beam can be obtained by contacting the women's gymnastic teacher at the local high school or college, or by reading in the competitive gymnastic books available in the library.

## VAULTING

Every child should experience jumping over boxes, bushes, or barrels. The mentally retarded child can learn to do this vaulting if the teaching is progressive, and if safety is kept positive at all times.

The vaulting box is an ideal piece of equipment. It can be lowered or raised as the performer gains skills. It is padded on top for safety and all of the parts store together.

Proper spotting techniques are essential for every vaulting activity. The spotter stands facing the vaulter and on the opposite side of the box. She is in a forward stride position with the arms up and forward. As the vaulter leaves the box, the spotter takes hold of the vaulter's nearest arm above and below the elbow and controls the vaulter as he leaves the box as he lands. In all of the following stunts the spotter will be in position and is to be actively spotting.

### Skill Progression

*Squat Vault*

The following skill progression is based on the squat vault:

1. Stand facing the box. Place the hands on the top of the box. Jump, lifting the hips and keeping the feet close to the box. The head is between the arms and the eyes are looking at the top of the box (Fig. 7-19).

2. Stand on the box and jump off.

3. Stand on the floor with the hands on the top of the box (box at midthigh level); jump and place the knees on the top of the box (Fig. 7-20). Stand up. Jump off.

4. Place the hands on the box and jump, placing the feet between the hands on the top of the box (Fig. 7-21). Stand up. Jump off.

5. Place the hands on the box. Jump and move the legs between the arms to the other side of the box and sit on the box (Fig. 7-22). Push on through and land on both feet.

6. Take four steps; place the hands on the box. Jump and place the feet on the top of the box. Push on through (Fig. 7-23) and land on the feet on the mat.

Figure 7-19                    Figure 7-20

Figure 7-21

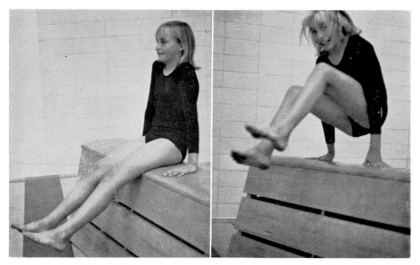

Figure 7-22                              Figure 7-23

7. Take a short run. Place the hands on the box. Jump and push legs through and land on the feet.

8. Take a longer run and repeat #7.

### Flank Vault

The flank vault is the basis for this skill progression:

1. Place the hands on the box. Swing both legs to the side and place them on the top of the box (Fig. 7-24). Push with the legs and swing them over the box. The spotter stands on the side of the jumper opposite the legs.

2. Place the hands on the box. Swing both legs completely over the box (Fig. 7-25) and land on the feet.

3. Take a short run. Swing the legs over the box and land on the feet.

4. Take a longer run. Swing the legs over the box and land on the feet.

### Wolf Vault

This skill progression is based on the wolf vault:

1. Place the hands on the box. Jump; swing one leg to the

Figure 7-24                         Figure 7-25

side as in the flank vault, one leg bending between the arms as in the squat vault. Land on the top of the box (Fig. 7-26). Push with feet and vault over the box. Land on the feet. The spotter is on the side of the vaulter opposite the extended leg.

Figure 7-26

2. Place the hands on the box. Do #1, but do not land on the top of the box.

3. Take a short run. Place the hands on the top of the box. Vault as described in #1.

4. Take a longer run. Vault as described in #1.

The vaulting box can also be used as a jumping box. The jumper stands on the top of the box and jumps from the box doing specific skills. Some of these are listed below:

1. Jump and do a half-turn.
2. Jump and do a full turn.
3. Jump and clap hands over the head.
4. Jump and turn and clap the hands over the head.
5. Jump and extend both legs forward.
6. Jump and bend both knees up to the chest.

In all of the activities of this chapter, safety must be stressed constantly. These activities are dangerous and care must be taken to protect the child from injury. Proper equipment must be provided. Mats are essential, and without them activities including stunts, tumbling, and apparatus should not be included. The expense may be great, but money can be made available for programs and mats, and equipment can be provided. It may be possible for equipment to be borrowed. The tumbling mats and other equipment are not in use constantly by the high schools, and special-education programs can use them during the "off season."

## ROPES

### Jumping Rope Skills

The physical fitness benefits received from jumping can hardly be matched in any other activity. Jumping rope is a part of childhood that is experienced by all children and is shared with them by adults. Every child can enjoy this activity and can share with others these joys of childhood.

A retarded child must know how to use the rope for jumping. He should not be allowed to use the rope for catching other children, or be allowed to swing or throw the rope at other children.

### Jumping Sequence for Single-Rope Skills

The following skill sequence involves the use of a short rope by a single child:

1. Practice jumping in place. Keep the rhythm even and use no rope.

2. Jump over a line on the floor. Keep the rhythm even and use no rope.

3. Place the rope on the floor. Jump over and back, keeping the rhythm even.

4. Hold one end of the rope in each hand. Place the rope in front of the toes and jump. Swing the rope overhead and back to the starting position.

5. Practice #4; keep the rope moving and continue jumping.

6. The child can progress to some of the more difficult single-rope skills. Crossed arms, backward jump, and crossed feet are examples.

### Long-Rope Learning Sequence

This skill sequence involves the use of a long rope by several children:

1. Stand side by side to a line. Jump over and back across the line.

2. Stand side by side to the rope. Jump over and back across the rope.

3. Two turners each hold an end and as the jumper jumps over they slowly swing the rope.

4. Practice #3, swinging the rope wider and wider.

5. Start standing by the rope. As the jumper jumps over, the turners turn the rope over his head and continue turning until the jumper misses.

6. The jumper is standing outside of the rope at the side of one of the turners. The teacher is next to the jumper and has hold of his hand. As the rope turns the teacher "hands" the jumper into the rope, being careful not to push him or jump in with him.

7. Practice #6 without "handing" the jumper in. The teacher should give verbal cues to show the jumper when to jump in.

8. The jumper leaves the rope as soon as he has jumped the designated number of jumps. Jump, run, and follow the rope is the motor pattern for getting out of the rope.

Children should include many of the rhymes of childhood that children all over the world know and love. Some of them are presented here. The neighborhood children are good sources for others.

Charlie Chaplin
Charles Chaplin went to France
To teach the ladies how to dance.
Heel and toe and away we go.
Heel and toe and away we go.
Bow to the captain,
Kneel to the queen,
And give a salute to the big Marine.

Charlie Chaplin
Charlie Chaplain sat on a pin.
How many inches did it go in?
1, 2, 3, 4, 5, . . .

Cinderella
Cinderella dressed in black
Went upstairs to peak through a crack.
How many people did she see?
1, 2, 3, 4, 5, . . .

Cinderella dressed in blue
Went upstairs to clean the flue.
How many flues did she clean?
1, 2, 3, 4, 5, . . .

Cinderella dressed in brown
Went upstairs to make a gown.
How many stitches did she use?
1, 2, 3, 4, 5, . . .

Cinderella dressed in red
Went upstairs to make the bed.
How many beds did she make?
1, 2, 3, 4, 5, . . .

Down by the Seashore
Susie broke the milk bottle
And blamed it onto me.
I told Ma,
Ma told Pa,
Susie got a licking
So ha ha ha.
How many lickings did she get?
1, 2, 3, 4, 5, . . .

Down in the Valley
Down in the valley where the green grass grows
Sat little Mary sweet as a rose.
Along came a billy goat
And kissed her on the nose.
How many kisses did she get?
1, 2, 3, 4, 5, . . .

Minny and a Minny
Minny and a minny and a ha ha ha,
Kissed her fellow on a Broadway car.
You tell Ma and I'll tell Pa,
Minny and a minny and a ha ha ha.

Raspberry
Raspberry, raspberry, raspberry jam,
Tell me the initials of your old man.
A, B, C, D, E, . . .

Strawberry Shortcake
Strawberry shortcake, cream of tartar,
Tell me the name of your sweethearter.

Teddy Bear
Teddy Bear, Teddy Bear, go up stairs;
Teddy Bear, Teddy Bear, say your prayers.
Teddy Bear, Teddy Bear, switch off the light;
Teddy Bear, Teddy Bear, say good night.

Verbalization experiences like the forenamed rhymes will help the child in his general conversation. The rhymes should be sung in a singsong rhythm and each of the children should be encouraged to participate in the singing, whether it is his turn or not.

## Other Rope Activities

### *Jumps*

The following are some additional rope activities involving jumping:

1. *High Jump.* Jump over a held rope. The rope is slowly raised after each child has had a turn.

2. *Long Jump.* After each child has had a turn slowly widen the distance between two ropes laid on the ground.

3. *Over and Under.* Two ropes are held parallel. The one closest to the jumper is held at knee height and the one farthest away is held at waist height. The child jumps the closest rope and rolls under the farthest rope. The highest of the two ropes is gradually reversed.

4. Zigzag the ropes.

### *Hanging Ropes*

Rope swings are among the activities provided by hanging ropes, as follows:

1. Sit on the knot and swing back and forth.
2. Stand on the knot and swing back and forth.
3. Increase the swing of the rope.
4. Climb onto a box, get on the rope, and swing.
5. Repeat #4 and at the height of the swing jump off.

Hanging ropes also provide opportunities for rope climbing, as described below:

1. Lie down under the rope and grasp the rope. Using a hand-over-hand movement, pull from lying position to a sitting position.

2. Lie down under the rope. Using a hand-over-hand movement, pull from lying position to a standing position.

3. Repeat #2 but return to lying position by slowly climbing down the rope. Keep the legs straight throughout the practice.

4. Stand on the knot with the rope between the legs, wrap the rope around to the back of the calf of the right leg, and under the arch of the right foot. Place the left foot on the top of the rope and next to the right foot (Fig. 7-27). Reach up the rope with the

Figure 7-27

hands. Bring the knees up toward the waist. Reach up the rope again with the hands. Repeat the leg action and continue up the rope. Climb down slowly, arms and then legs. Do *not* slide. A climber should save enough energy to climb down the rope. He should not expend all of his energy in the climb up.

A retarded child should be told how high to climb and he should be spotted throughout the activity. The rope can be painted to designate different heights. The child should be talked to and encouraged to go only to the predetermined height.

# Chapter 8

# LOW-ORGANIZATIONAL GAMES

THE BENEFITS to the mentally retarded child from functioning in a group cannot be underrated. So very often the retarded child is isolated and is not included in family group experiences or in the neighborhood group experiences. There are many reasons why he is left out of these activities, but nevertheless he needs group experiences in order to develop to his full potential. We hear mothers of normal children talk about how important it is for their child to have other children with whom to play, and for their child to learn about sharing from these other children. These mothers often go to great lengths to arrange for children to meet in groups for this needed growth experience. The retarded child has equal needs for small-group association experiences. Games of low organization can help serve this need. Group games for all children can teach the children involved to get along with each other without argument, to cooperate with each other, to have fun in a group, and to be an accepted member of a group or team. A mixed group of retardates and normal children will be a structured group, especially set up for teaching the normal children to be understanding and compassionate. The retardate will benefit from association with normal children and from association with other retarded children. They all can function together in this situation.

Games included in this section are selected with organizations simple enough to be easily understood, uncomplicated rules, and low excitement levels. The retarded or emotionally disturbed child often cannot participate in active, exciting games of chasing or throwing. Many of the games included here require verbalization by the children. This type of game should be encouraged so that the child becomes accustomed to responding. This can help him in general conversation with other persons with whom he comes in contact.

### Cat and Mouse

*Formation.* Children seated in a circle.

*Equipment.* Two different-colored bean bags.

*Number of Players.* Small group, six to eight children.

*Game.* One bean bag is called the mouse and is passed around the circle. The other bean bag is called the cat and is passed around the circle in the same direction. When the cat catches the mouse the game is over.

### Circus

*Formation.* Single circle with one child in the center.

*Equipment.* None.

*Number of Players.* Six to eight children.

*Game.* The child in the center is the ringmaster and moves around the inside of the circle calling out names of animals. The circle children imitate the sounds of the animals. The leader calls out, "Join the parade." All of the children march around behind the ringmaster acting like the animals.

The teacher may have to be the ringmaster.

### Duck Duck Goose

*Formation.* Single circle with children seated. One child is standing outside the circle.

*Equipment.* None.

*Number of Players.* Six to eight children.

*Game.* The child outside the circle runs around the circle, touches one child and says "Duck," touches another child and says "Duck," touches a third child and says *"Goose."* The goose chases "It" around the circle to the "Goose's" position in the circle. If "It" is tagged, he is "It" again. If "It" gets to the place, he stays there and the other player becomes "It."

### Objects Go Around

*Formation.* Single circle with children seated.

*Equipment.* Three or four different-shaped objects and a record player or piano.

*Number of Players.* Eight to ten children.

*Game.* Objects are distributed around the circle. Music starts and the players pass the objects all in the same direction. The object of the game is not to have an object in your possession when the music stops.

## Ball Counting

*Formation.* Single circle with the children seated.

*Equipment.* Large playground ball.

*Number of Players.* Eight to ten children.

*Game.* The teacher rolls the ball acrosss the circle; a child catches it and says "one." He then rolls the ball across the circle to another child, who says "two." The object of the game is for the group to get as high a count as it can. If rolling the ball is too easy, the children should be standing and the ball may be thrown.

The leader should make certain that no child is left out.

## Go, Go, Go, Stop

*Formation.* Children in a single line with a leader twenty feet in front with his back to the group.

*Equipment.* None.

*Number of Players.* Eight to ten children.

*Game.* Leader says "Go, go, go" and continues saying "Go" as the children advance toward the end line. The leader says "Stop" and turns around. The children all stop. If any child is moving after "Stop," that child goes back to the starting line.

The teacher may need to be the leader for this game.

## Jump the Brook

*Formation.* Single line of children. Two chalk lines are drawn in front of the children. The chalk lines gradually widen.

*Equipment.* None.

*Number of Players.* Eight to ten children.

*Game.* Each child looks over the brook and decides where he can safely run and jump across without getting his feet wet. When all of the children are over, they each jump again. The children should be encouraged to jump at a wider spot each time.

## Jump the Shot

*Formation.* Single circle with a leader in the center.

*Equipment.* A long rope with a towel, sock, or boxing glove tied to one end .

*Number of Players.* Eight to ten children.

*Game.* Leader swings the rope so that the "shot" is close to the floor and swings around the circle. The children jump over the shot as it comes close to them. If they miss, it is only a miss; no one is eliminated from the game. At the end of the game, all children who did not miss are honored.

## Bowling

*Formation.* Single circle.

*Equipment.* Three bowling pins, empty milk cartons or plastic bottles, and two small playground balls.

*Number of Players.* Three to four children.

*Game.* Players take turns trying to knock over the pins by rolling the balls. One ball is rolled at the three pins. The second ball is rolled at any pins left standing. Each child retrieves his own balls and sets up the pins for the next bowler.

## Cut the Cake

*Formation.* Single circle with one child in the center.

*Equipment.* None.

*Number of Players.* Eight to ten children.

*Game.* The children in the circle join hands. The child in the center raises his hand over his head (the knife) . He *gently* brings his hand down over the joined hands of two circle players (cuts the cake). The children run in opposite directions around the outside of the circle. The first one back into place is the new knife and the game continues.

Other games played on the playground or in the gymnasium can be taught to the mentally retarded children. By teaching the retardate the same games that are being played by the normal children in his neighborhood, his chances of being accepted by the group are increased. Some of these games played throughout the nation are "Red Rover," "Red Light, Green Light," "Here

Comes a Jolly Butcher Boy," and "I Have a Little Dog and He Won't Bite You."

## Teaching Suggestions

The teacher of the above games will find the following suggestions useful:

1. The teacher should play an active role in the game. He should be a part of the game by being the leader or by helping each child take his part. As soon as a child can take the leadership position he should be encouraged to do so.

2. The teacher should get the children into the formation to be used for the game before any explanation or demonstration is given.

3. The teacher should talk to each child as his turn comes. He should encourage him to be ready and he should assist him to succeed.

4. The teacher should have the class play the game only as long as the interest level is high. A child's attention span can be increased with the use of games, and this can carry over into other learning situations.

# Chapter 9

# SEQUENTIAL DEVELOPMENT OF
# SPORT SKILLS

O NE OF THE EDUCATIONAL objectives of a program of instruction in special education is to help the children learn to live with their families and to function in society as well as possible. Participation in sports is part of life in our society. Family recreation activities usually involve sport skills and related games and most neighborhood play centers around these same types of games. It is for the child with learning disabilities that the following approach toward sequential development of sport skills is designed. The handicapped child needs to learn the skills that normal children know if he is to associate with normal children. What is more important to a normal child than to be able to throw and catch a ball and participate in the neighborhood games? It is also important that the handicapped child possess the skills necessary to be accepted in the group activity.

The slow learner is mainly self-centered. His self-image and what he thinks others think of him dictate to a great extent his potential for learning and his participation in activity. The special child wants to increase his own ability so he can participate with the normal children and in his own peer group. When he learns a skill he gains confidence because he can do a skill which normal children do. He may not do it as well, but he can still say, "I can do it." He may be able to make one out of twenty-five shots at the basket, but he can make that one.

The purpose of this approach for teaching the basic sport skills is to simplify the skills, to provide skill games of a simple nature which can be used to practice these skills, and to provide gradual involvement in the lead-up to sport games and the sport games themselves. The main concern is with the simplification of the skills and the beginning aspects of the game involvement.

The analytical process of the skill will vary according to the characteristics of the child or group. It should be individualized to meet each child's needs. A basic premise which should be remembered when we teach skills to the slow learner is to plan for guaranteed successes. Start at that point at which the participant is successful, then reinforce this success and progress to the next step. All activities need to be adapted to the potential of the individual. He needs to feel success and be motivated to continue to improve his ability.

Satisfaction is a primary factor in motivation and it is especially necessary for the handicapped. Because of the short attention span, the satisfaction needs to come early. Praise from the teacher is particularly appreciated. Retarded children are *object bound*—problems or games involving success with objects are particularly effective motivators for them. A good example of this is the popularity of bowling as an activity among the retarded.

The use of imitation is one of the most effective means of teaching the retarded. Kinesthetic movement is another effective method of teaching skills. This would suggest the use of audiovisual aids, exploration, and sound-teaching techniques.

Incidental learning is low among the retarded. They cannot surmise for themselves that a good follow-through will give force and direction to an overhand throw. The basic principles of movement need to be observed in practice and reinforced to provide for good skill performance. It is imperative for the retarded child to learn the skill correctly so that relearning it is not necessary.

One of the typical movement problems is to convince the handicapped to use all body parts in the movement. Many retarded students, particularly the trainable, tire easily and therefore expand as little energy as possible. Others have not been encouraged to use their bodies, but rather have been encouraged to sit quietly and not be a disturbance. These children use as little motion as possible. A throw for a retarded youngster usually involves the use of the arm only. As a result the power and distance of the throw is limited.

Other teaching suggestions which may be helpful are listed below.

1. Begin by using large balls and gradually reduce the size of the ball used.

2. Teach a ready position to be used to catch, dodge, or chase.

3. Most skills, will be more efficiently performed when opposition in the movement is used; for example, "Step out with the foot opposite the throwing hand."

4. For the handicapped the ability to exert force is difficult to acquire. Proper timing of movement, muscular strength, and momentum are factors to observe where force is lacking. Proper timing is movement at the proper moment; for example, "Step as you throw." Momentum is developed by increasing the distance of the preparatory movement, such as rotation in a throw. Force is also increased by increasing the speed of the movement.

5. The follow-through is also important in the action. If the movement stops too soon the speed is reduced and less momentum is imparted to the object. Lack of follow-through will also affect the direction of the action or the ball.

6. Focus on the object of the action; for example, "Keep your eye on the ball."

7. Change the rules and equipment to fit the situation; for example, a deflated ball is easier to handle than a fully inflated one.

8. Try to make the situation and practice as much like the regular game as possible so that the retarded will be able to participate in a normal activity.

9. The interest span of the children is short; therefore activities should be changed often.

10. The retarded child lacks a knowledge of basic skills, such as a pivot or a dodge, so these need to be taught specifically.

The following ball handling skills are presented with a brief description of the skill, a progressive list of practice drills, several simple skill games for each skill, and games which are enjoyed by normal children. The beginning drills and skill games are for those children who have not had any experience with ball handling activities. Children who have played games in their neighborhood or who have had school experiences would be ready for

## GAME SKILLS PROFICIENCY RECORD

Name _____ Age _____

*Date*

| | | | |
|---|---|---|---|
| Roll a ball between partner's legs. | | | |
| Roll a ball against the wall and catch it. | | | |
| Bounce and catch a ball with a partner. | | | |
| Bounce a ball with either hand. | | | |
| Bounce a ball while running. | | | |
| Bounce a ball around several objects. | | | |
| Catch a utility ball from a throw ten feet away. | | | |
| Catch a nine-inch ball from twenty feet away. | | | |
| Catch a softball. | | | |
| Throw a ball with an underhand toss. | | | |
| Throw a ball with a chest pass. | | | |
| Throw a ball or bean bag into a wastebasket. | | | |
| Throw a ball twenty feet. | | | |
| Kick a stationary ball. | | | |
| Kick a rolling ball. | | | |
| Run and kick a stationary ball. | | | |
| Run and kick a rolling ball. | | | |
| Kick a ball twenty feet. | | | |
| Dribble a ball using both feet. | | | |
| Hit a ball off a batting tee. | | | |
| Hit a thrown ball. | | | |
| Hit a volleyball with an underhand hit. | | | |
| Hit a volleyball with an overhand hit. | | | |
| Serve a volleyball. | | | |
| Make a two-hand underhand BB shot. | | | |
| Make a chest shot or a one-hand shot. | | | |
| Throw a softball sixty feet. | | | |
| Catch a bouncing softball. | | | |
| Hit a target with an underhand pitch. | | | |
| Hit a target with an overhand throw. | | | |

more advanced practice drills. Other children may be more advanced and may be ready to participate in the activities of normal school children. Learning concepts from other areas of the curriculum, such as communication, have been incorporated into the skill games as an example of an integrated learning situation.

A Game Skills Proficiency Record is included as an aid for the teacher to subjectively evaluate the child's skill performance. The purpose of the chart is to show the performance ability of the individual on a specific date. The skill items can be performed periodically and the results compared to evaluate improvement. An evaluative term recorded on the child's performance record for each skill will help to compare performances on succeeding dates. The usual terms of "excellent," "good," "average," or "poor" may be supplemented with description of the analysis, such as "poor body involvement," "average accuracy," "good focus," and so forth. The teacher may add objective measures of performance for each skill which would be appropriate for the child or type of children with whom he works. For instance, a specific number of trials may be listed for each skill and the number of successful attempts recorded. Example: Throw the softball twenty feet; score, six out of ten attempts were successful.

## BEAN BAG SKILLS

The following list of skills is arranged progressively:

1. Using an underhand toss, throw a bean bag to a partner.

2. Using an underhand toss, throw a bean bag into the air and catch it. Gradually toss it higher.

3. Toss a bean bag into the air, clap hands together, and catch the bean bag.

4. Toss a bean bag so it lands in a circle on the floor eight or ten feet away.

5. Toss a bean bag into a wastebasket.

6. Using two bean bags, toss one bean bag to partner and catch the one the partner has thrown.

7. Using an underhand toss, throw a bean bag at a small target (bowling pin on a chair) .

8. Throw a bean bag with an overhand toss to a partner.

9. Throw a bean bag as far as possible. Run and pick it up.

10. Toss the bean bag into the air, turn around, and catch it.

11. Throw a bean bag so it lands in a circle twenty feet distant.

12. Throw a bean bag at a target fifteen feet away.

### Teaching Suggestions

Listed below are some suggestions for the teacher of bean-bag skills:

1. A bean bag, a stuffed stocking, or a yarn ball is easier to catch and throw than a ball; therefore, it is wise to begin practice in throwing and catching with one of these items. It will also provide more practice in throwing and catching since a missed bean bag does not roll away.

2. Beginning players will usually use two hands.

3. Do not be too concerned with the mechanics of the throw at first, but emphasize catching with both hands and let them become familiar with the bean bag and the action.

4. After some experience, most children will begin to continually use a dominant hand instead of both hands.

5. When the majority of the participants are using one hand, emphasize correct stance and action.

## Bean Bag Skill Games

### Kitten in a Basket

*Formation.* Semicircle at the starting line. Place a wastebasket or box six feet in front of each team.

*Equipment.* Five stuffed stockings (kittens) and one box or wastebasket for each team.

*Number of Players.* Five or six on each team.

*Game.* Each child is given five consecutive throws at the basket. Each time the kitten lands in the basket the children all repeat together "One kitten in the basket" or "Two kittens in the basket" and so on. After each player completes his last throw he collects the kittens, gives them to the next player, and returns to his position in the semicircle. The player or team with the highest number of kittens in the basket wins.

*Teaching Suggestions.* As skill improves use bean bags and increase the distance or make the basket smaller.

*Kitten on the Fence*

*Formation.* A column formation behind the throwing line.

*Equipment.* A stool or balance beam with a stuffed stocking or stuffed kitten on it. One bean bag for each player.

*Number of Players.* Five or six in each group.

*Game.* Each child is given one throw at the kitten. If he succeeds in knocking the kitten off the fence, he runs up and places it back on the fence and returns with his bean bag. Each child must run up, get his bean bag, and return to the end of the column before the next player may throw. The child or the team with the most hits wins the game.

*Teaching Suggestions.* To simplify the game one kitten for each child may be placed on the fence. The bean bags may stay until the game is over to avoid confusion.

## BALL EXERCISES

The following exercise using balls are suggested:

1. Reach up high while holding the ball.
2. Hold the ball at arm's length and twist from side to side.
3. Place a ball by the toes and pick it up. Keep the legs straight.
4. Roll a ball around the feet.
5. Make a figure eight by rolling a ball in and out of feet.
6. Run while carrying the ball.
7. Sit up while a ball is held in different positions.
8. Jump over a stationary ball.

## BALL ROLLING SKILLS

*Two-Hand Front Roll, Sitting.* Partners sit on the floor and roll the ball back and forth, using both hands to push and catch the ball.

*Two-Hand Front Roll, Standing.* Partners roll the ball back and forth while in a standing position. The ball should be held with the fingertips, one hand on each side of the ball. The backswing goes between the legs. The action is forward toward the partner. Release the ball near the floor. Follow through toward the partner.

*Two-Hand Side Roll, Right Side.* Stand with the left foot forward in a front-stride position. The ball is held in both hands. The ball is brought back on the right side and forward toward the partner, releasing the ball near the floor.

*Two-Hand Side Roll, Left Side.* Stand with the right foot forward in a front-stride position. The ball is brought back on the left side and forward toward the partner, releasing the ball near the floor.

*One-Hand Roll.* Place the left foot forward, knees bent; hold the ball in the right hand in front of the body. Swing the arm backward and forward, stepping with the left foot as the ball comes forward. Release the ball near the ground and follow through toward the target.

### Ball Rolling Progression and Drills

The drills that follow are listed progressively:

1. While sitting with the legs spread sideways, roll the ball to a partner.
2. While seated, roll the ball against the wall.
3. While standing, roll the ball forward, run after and stop it.
4. Roll the ball through a partner's legs.
5. Roll the ball at partner's foot (Fig. 9-1).

Figure 9-1

6. Roll the ball along a painted line.
7. Roll the ball into a box.
8. Roll the ball at a pin six to fifteen feet away.
9. Roll the ball backwards through the legs.
10. Do a two-hand side roll on the right side.
11. Do a two-hand side roll on the left side.
12. Do a one-hand roll.
13. Roll the ball, run and jump over it.
14. Roll the ball for distance.

## Ball Rolling Skill Games

### Roll Call

*Formation.* Fan formation.

Teacher

*Equipment.* Utility ball (9 or 13 inches).

*Number of Players.* Four to six in each group.

*Game.* One child is chosen to be "It" for each group. He assumes a position fifteen feet in front of the group. "It" rolls the ball in front of the group. After catching the ball, the called player one of his group. The called player runs forward and catches the ball in front of the group. After catching the ball, the called player rolls the ball back to "It." The game continues until all the children's names have been called by "It," or until the teacher designates a time limit. Each child is given an opportunity to be "It."

*Teaching Suggestions.* The teacher should be "It" until the children understand the game.

The child who is "It" may need help in remembering all the children's names. Also, the other children may need to have their names called before the ball is rolled to them to get their attention.

### Leader Ball

*Formation.* Fan formation.

Leader

*Equipment.* Utility ball (9 or 13 inches).

*Number of Players.* Six to ten in each group.

*Game.* One child is chosen to be the "Leader." He stands fifteen feet in front of the group. The "Leader" rolls the ball to the player at the head of the line, who stops the ball and rolls it back to the "Leader." The "Leader" repeats the action to each player. The last player stops the ball and runs with the ball to become the new "Leader," while all the children call his name and say, for example, "Randy is the new Leader."

*Teaching Suggestions.* First, verbalization is important for all children. Secondly, with several groups, the game can be a relay.

### Circle Ball

*Formation.* Single circle with children facing the center.

*Equipment.* Utility ball (9 or 13 inches).

*Number of Players.* Eight to twelve.

*Game.* Players take a kneeling or stooping position in the circle. To start the game, the teacher rolls a ball into the circle. When the ball rolls to a player, he stops it and tries to roll it between two other circle players. If the ball rolls out of the circle, the player who rolled the ball stands and performs a stunt related to the classroom activity of the day.

*Teaching Suggestion.* Integrate the subject matter into the classroom, such as a rhyme or chant to reinforce learning and encourage verbalization.

### Break the Circle

*Formation.* Single circle with children facing the center.

*Equipment.* Utility ball (9 or 13 inches).

*Number of Players.* Ten to twelve.

*Game.* One child is chosen to be "It." He assumes a position in the center of the circle. The children in the circle assume a stride position with the outer edges of their feet touching the player next to them. "It" attempts to "break the circle" by rolling the ball between the legs of any circle player or between any two players. If the circle player can catch the ball, he becomes "It."

*Teaching Suggestion.* Have the children facing away from the circle. The ball must be rolled through the legs.

### Roll Dodge Ball

*Formation.* Single circle with children facing the center.

*Equipment.* Utility ball (9 or 13 inches).

*Number of Players.* Ten to twelve.

*Game.* One child is chosen to be "It." He assumes a position in the center of the circle. The children in the circle try to roll the ball at the feet of the player who is "It." "It" must stay within a two-foot circle. He may jump or slide within the circle to avoid being hit.

Circle players may enter the circle to retrieve the ball; however, they may not throw at any opponent until they join the edge of the circle. If the circle player can hit "It," he then becomes "It" and the former "It" joins the circle.

*Teaching Suggestion.* If the circle players have difficulty hitting "It," use two or more balls.

### King's Guard

*Formation.* Single circle with the children facing the center.

*Equipment.* Utility ball (9 or 13 inches) and one bowling pin.

*Number of Players.* Eight to twelve.

*Game.* Place the bowling pin in the center of the circle. One child is chosen to be the "King's Guard." Circle players roll the ball and attempt to knock down the bowling pin while the "King's Guard" tries to prevent the ball from hitting the "king pin." King's Guard" may stop the ball by blocking it with his legs or catching it. If the "King's Guard" accidently knocks down the "king pin" or the ball knocks down the "king pin," the circle player who last threw the ball becomes the "King's Guard".

*Teaching Suggestions.* A circle drawn on the floor for the pin will help to keep it centered. A circle on the floor for the circle players will help them maintain the proper size of circle.

### Three-Pin Bowling

*Formation.* The class is in a column behind the starting line.

```
                                                        o
     xxxx         . . . . . . . . . . . . . . . . . . . . . . . . .   o
                                                        o
```

*Equipment.* Three bowling pins and a utility ball or a rubber bowling ball.

*Number of Players.* Four to six in each group.

*Game.* Two children are chosen to set the pins and return the balls. Each child is given two attempts to knock the pins down. Each child adds his pin total on the blackboard after each turn. The child with the highest total after ten turns is the winner.

Children take turns setting up the pins and returning the balls.

*Teaching Suggestions.* Circles drawn on the floor for the bowling pins will help the children to place them in a proper triangular shape. The ball should be rolled from the side of the body.

### Ten-Pin Bowling

Adapt official rules to meet the situation. Use a large space.

### BALL BOUNCING SKILLS

*Two-Hand Bounce.* Hold the ball in the fingertips. Extend the arms downward and slightly forward and push the ball with the fingertips. The hands meet the ball on the rebound and give with the ball as it comes up. The fingertips serve as a cushion as the ball rebounds and is pushed down.

*One-Hand Bounce.* Hold the ball in the left hand with the right hand on top of the ball. The weight is on both feet with the knees slightly bent. Extend the forearm downward and slightly forward and push the ball toward the floor with the fingertips. As the ball rebounds, the fingertips, wrist, and elbow give. The cushion is ready to rebound the ball back to the floor with a pumping action from the elbow (Fig. 9-2).

Figure 9-2

## Ball Bouncing Progression and Drills

The following drills are listed progressively:

1. Using two hands, bounce the ball to yourself and catch it.

2. Using two hands, bounce the ball two or three times and catch it.

3. Using two hands, bounce the ball to a partner.

4. Still using both bands, bounce the ball hard and catch it as it comes down.

5. Bounce the ball with one hand.

6. Bounce the ball with the other hand.

7. Bounce the ball several times with one hand.

8. Bounce the ball several times using one hand and two hands alternately.

9. Bounce the ball while walking.

10. Bounce the ball while running.

11. Bounce the ball, clap the hands, and catch the ball.

12. Bounce the ball in rhythm.

13. Bounce the ball, turn around, and catch the ball.

14. Bounce the ball in a circle so it rebounds to a partner.

15. Bounce the ball in a target several times (hopscotch maze).

16. While bouncing the ball, swing one leg over the ball (Fig. 9-3).

17. Bounce the ball around, behind, and back to the front and catch the ball (Fig. 9-4).

18. Bounce the ball several times on the right side, bounce to the left side, and bounce the ball several times on the left side without stopping.

19. Keep the ball bouncing while assuming a sitting position (Fig. 9-5), then a lying position. Return to standing position.

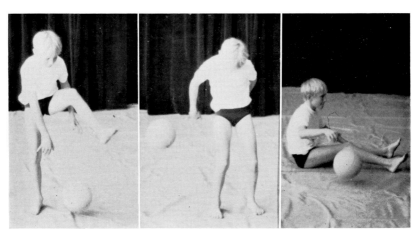

Figure 9-3              Figure 9-4              Figure 9-5

## Ball Bouncing Skill Games

### Circle Bounce Ball

*Formation.* Single circle with the children facing the center.

*Equipment.* Utility ball (9 or 13 inches).

*Number of Players.* Six to twelve.

*Game.* One child is chosen to be in the center of the circle. The center player bounces the ball to a circle player, who returns it with a bounce pass also. The center player continues to bounce the ball around the circle until all circle players have had a turn. After completing his turn in the circle, the circle player chooses a new center player.

*Teaching Suggestions.* All players should have a turn in the center of the circle. Also, two balls and two center players may be used for more advanced children.

### Fifteen Bounces

*Formation.* Single circle with the children facing the center.
*Equipment.* Utility ball (9 or 13 inches).
*Number of Players.* Four to eight per group.
*Game.* One player stands in the circle with the ball. The center player attempts to bounce the ball fifteen times in succession. If the center player misses the ball before completing fifteen bounces, the child in the circle who retrieves the ball goes to the center and attempts to complete fifteen bounces. If the center player completes fifteen bounces, he selects the next child to become the center player.

All the children in the circle count the bounces for the center player.

*Teaching Suggestions.* All players should have a turn in the center of the circle. Encourage all children to count, too.

Use all available balls.

### Bouncing Ball

*Formation.* Single circle with the children facing the center.
*Equipment.* Utility ball (9 or 13 inches).
*Number of Players.* Five to ten.
*Game.* One child is selected to start the game in the center of the circle. The center player begins the game by bouncing the ball several times. While bouncing the ball he calls the name of a circle player. The called child runs to the center of the circle and, without losing the bounce, keeps the ball bouncing. Play continues until all children have had a turn bouncing the ball. Try to decrease the number of errors each time the game is played.

*Teaching Suggestion.* The first time the children play the game, let them use two hands. Gradually progress toward using only one hand to hit the ball.

**Number Bounce**

*Formation.* Single column behind the starting line.

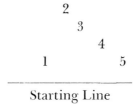

Starting Line

*Equipment.* Utility ball (9 or 13 inches).

*Number of Players.* Four to eight.

*Game.* The first player in the column walks to circle number one, bounces the ball once, catches the ball, and walks to circle two and bounces the ball twice. He continues through all five circles. The second player begins when the first player finishes. The first player goes to the end of the column. Play continues until all children have finished the maze. The children who complete the maze without a mistake write their names on the blackboard or lead the class in a rhyme or song.

*Teaching Suggestion.* The children should help the performer count in each square.

**Target Bouncing**

*Formation.* Single circle with children facing the center.

*Equipment.* Utility ball (9 or 13 inches).

*Number of Players.* Six to twelve in each group.

*Game.* A three-foot circle is drawn in the center of each circle of children. The children in the circle attempt to bounce the ball in the center circle on the floor. One point is earned each time the ball lands in the center circle. The group with the most points after a designated time limit wins.

*Teaching Suggestion.* Points can be counted for each child rather than group competition. The group could compete against itself by attempting to improve the group score each time the game is played.

## CATCHING SKILLS

*Catching with Arms and Body.* The arms are held in front of the body in a partially bent position. The fingers are spread and curved. The arms and body make a "basket." As the ball comes, line up with the ball so it lands in the "basket." Give with all parts of the body and bring the ball to the body as it is caught (Fig. 9-6).

*Catching with Hands and Body.* The hands are cupped with the palms up. The fingers are spread and the arms partially extended. Grasp the ball with the hands and pull the ball to the body. Give with the ball as it is caught. The ball remains largely in the hands (Fig. 9-7).

Figure 9-6

Figure 9-7

*Catching with Hands.* The fingers are curved and slightly relaxed. The hands and arms extend to meet the ball. Give with the ball as it is caught. If the ball is chest high or higher, the thumbs are together, the fingers spread, and the palms are turned away from the body (Fig. 9-8). If the ball is waist high or below, the little fingers are together with the palms up.

Figure 9-8

## Catching Skill Progression

The following catching skills are listed progressively:

1. With the arms and body, catch a simple toss from a partner.

2. Toss the ball to yourself and catch it with the arms and body.

3. Using the hands and body, catch a toss from a partner.

4. Using the hands, catch a toss from a partner.

5. Toss the ball high and catch the ball after it bounces.

6. Catch a toss with the hands.

7. Using the hands, catch a throw from a partner.

8. Catch a bouncing ball.

9. Catch a moving bouncing ball.

10. Catch a long pass.

11. Catch a pass while moving.

## Catching Skill Games

### Circle Pass

*Formation.* Single circle with the children facing the ball.

*Equipment.* Utility ball (9 or 13 inches).

*Number of Players.* Six to ten.

*Game.* Each child faces the ball. The player with the ball passes the ball to the player on his right. After catching the ball, each player faces the player on his right and passes the ball to the next player. Play continues until the ball reaches the starting point.

*Teaching Suggestions.* Change direction after completing the circle. Time the group and try to improve the length of time it takes the group to complete the circle.

## Circle Call Ball

*Formation.* Single circle with children facing the center.
*Equipment.* Utility ball (9 or 13 inches).
*Number of Players.* Ten to twelve.
*Game.* One child is chosen to be "It." "It" tosses the ball in the air and simultaneously calls the name of a circle player. The circle player must catch the ball while it is in the circle. If the circle player catches the ball, he becomes "It." If the circle player fails to catch the ball, "It" remains in the circle and calls another name as he tosses the ball.

*Teaching Suggestion.* As the players improve their catching ability, require them to catch it after one or two bounces. Progress until the children are able to catch it before it bounces.

The children may need help to remember the names of all the other children.

## Teacher Call Ball

*Formation.* Single circle with the children facing the center of the circle.
*Equipment.* Utility ball (9 or 13 inches).
*Number of Players.* Eight to twelve.
*Game.* The teacher is in the center of the circle. The teacher tosses the ball into the air and calls the name of one player. The called player attempts to catch the ball after one bounce. After catching the ball, the called player throws it back to the teacher.

*Teaching Suggestions.* As the skill of the players improves, (a) the children should attempt to catch the ball before it bounces and (b) allow the child who caught the ball to be "It."

## THROWING SKILLS

*Two-Hand Underhand Throw (Toss).* Weight is on both feet with the knees slightly bent. The feet are spread. The ball is held by the fingers with both hands slightly under the ball. The throw begins with a backswing between the legs and continues forward and upward as the arms extend. The follow-through is in the direction of the throw (Fig. 9-9) .

Figure 9-9

*Two-Hand Side Throw.* Stand with the left foot forward. The ball is held by the fingers of both hands. The ball is held in front of the body. The throw begins with a backswing to the right side as the weight is transferred to the right foot. The action continues forward. As the arms extend toward the target, the weight is transferred to the left foot (Fig. 9-10) .

*Two-Hand Chest Throw.* Stand with the feet apart and one foot slightly forward. The ball is held by the fingers at chest level. Elbows are bent and close to the sides. Thumbs are behind the ball with fingers spread. Move the weight forward as the arms extend forward toward the target. Snap the wrists (Fig. 9-11) .

*One-Hand Shoulder Throw.* The left foot is forward. The ball is held by the fingers in front of the body. Bring the arms back, transferring the ball to the right hand when it is above the right shoulder and behind the ear. The body rotates to the right. Shift

Figure 9-10

the weight to the right foot. Rotate the body and whip the arm forward, shifting the body weight forward. Release the ball with a wrist snap (Fig. 9-12).

*Underhand Throw (Pitching)*. Hold the ball by the fingers in front of the body with both hands. The throw begins with a back-swing downward and backwards. Transfer the ball to the right hand. The body rotates to the right. Swing the right arm forward, rotate the shoulders forward, and step forward on the left foot. Follow through in the direction of the ball (Fig. 9-13).

Figure 9-11                                    Figure 9-12

Figure 9-13

*Overhand Throw.* Stand with the left foot forward. Hold the ball by the fingers in front of the body. Twist the body to the right as the ball is brought backward and upward behind the ear. Swing right arm forward toward the target as shoulders rotate forward. Step on the left foot as the action continues forward. Release the ball off the fingers with a wrist snap (Fig. 9-14).

Figure 9-14

### Throwing Skill Progression
The throwing skills listed below are arranged progressively:
1. Two-hand underhand throw to partner.
2. Two-hand underhand throw to self.

3. Underhand throw into a box six feet away.

4. Underhand throw at a target on the wall six to thirteen feet away.

5. Underhand throw into the air, clap hands, and catch.

6. Underhand throw into the air, turn around, and catch.

7. Two-hand side throw on right side to partner.

8. Two-hand side throw on left side to partner.

9. Two-hand chest throw to partner.

10. One-hand shoulder throw to partner.

11. Underhand throw to partner.

12. Overhand throw to partner.

13. Throw to wall and catch the ball.

14. Count the number of consecutive throws and catches without an error.

15. Throw at a target on the wall.

16. Combine a bounce with all types of throws while throwing to a partner.

17. Throw the ball for distance.

18. Throw to a moving target.

## Throwing Skill Games

### Circle Toss Ball

*Formation.* Single circle with the children facing the center of the circle.

*Equipment.* Utility ball.

*Number of Players.* Six to ten.

*Game.* The ball is tossed across the circle from child to child. Encourage throws across the circle rather than around the circle. Count the number of passes without a miss. The count starts over after each miss. Keep a record of the group's performance and try to improve their score each time the game is played.

*Teaching Suggestion.* Begin by using an underhand throw. As the skill of the group improves, use other types of throws.

### Target Ball

*Formation.* Single circle with the children facing the center of the circle.

*Equipment.* Two utility balls of different color.

*Number of Players.* Eight to twelve.

*Game.* One ball is placed on a box in the center of the circle. The circle players throw the other ball at the "target" ball, attempting to hit it off the box. When a player knocks the ball off the box, he runs around the circle once while the teacher or a helper replaces the ball on the box.

Make provision for equal turns for each child.

*Teaching Suggestions.* Allow those children who have difficulty in hitting the target ball to help in replacing the ball on the box.

Begin by using an underhand throw. As the skill of the group improves, use other types of throws.

### Hit the Star

*Formation.* Column behind the throwing line.

*Equipment.* Utility ball and a star wall target.

*Number of Players.* Five to six per group.

*Game.* Each child is given one throw at the target each turn. Each time a child hits the star he is given a star to paste by his name on an achievement chart. Each child should have at least three tries before the game ends.

*Teaching Suggestion.* Start with an underhand throw. As the skill of the group improves, use other types of throws.

### One-Base Throw

*Formation.* One person with the ball at home base while the rest of the class is in the field around first base, fifteen to twenty feet from home base.

*Equipment.* Utility ball and two bases.

*Number of Players.* Six to ten.

*Game.* The player at home base throws the ball with a two-hand side throw into the playing area and runs to first base and back home. The players in the field attempt to get the ball and run home with it before the runner returns home. If the fielder tags home base before the runner returns home, the runner becomes a fielder. A fielder who has not had a turn becomes the thrower at home base.

*Teaching Suggestion.* If the child at home base is better skilled than the other players, have him throw the ball under his leg before running.

## Pin Guard

*Formation.* Single circle with the children facing the center of the circle.

*Equipment.* Bowling pin and a utility ball.

*Number of Players.* Eight to twelve.

*Game.* One child stands in the center to guard the pin. The circle players attempt to knock the pin down down by hitting it with the ball. If the circle player knocks the pin over he becomes the "pin guard." The guard may use his hands, feet, legs, or body in protecting the pin. If the guard knocks the pin over while attempting to protect it, he changes places with the circle player who threw the last ball.

*Teaching Suggestion.* Begin by using an underhand throw. As the skill of the group improves, use different types of throws.

## One-Man Dodge Ball

*Formation.* Single circle with the children facing the center of the circle.

*Equipment.* Utility ball.

*Number of Players.* Six to ten.

*Game.* One player is selected to be "It." He assumes a position in the center of the circle. The players in the circle attempt to hit "It" below the shoulders. If the circle player is successful and hits "It," the circle player then becomes "It." After the children become familiar with the game, count the number of throws the circle player requires to hit "It."

*Teaching Suggestion.* Begin by using an underhand throw. As the skill of the group improves, use different types of throws.

### Three-Man Dodge Ball

*Formation.* One third of the class on each end line and the other third of the class on the center line.

*Equipment.* One utility ball for each set of three players.

*Number of Players.* Three to thirty.

*Game.* Group an end-line player from each end with a center-line player. Each group of three should be at least five feet from the next group. The two end-line players in the group of three throw the ball at the center-line player, attempting to hit him below the waist. When an end-line player succeeds in hitting the center-line player, he then becomes the center-line player and the center-line player becomes an end-line player.

*Teaching Suggestions.* Begin by using underhand throw and progress to an overhand throw.

Players staying on the center-line the longest may move to the top of the line and be regrouped, thus equalizing the competition.

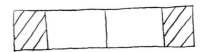

### Goal-Line Ball

*Formation.* Rectangular area with a center line drawn width-wise. Children are divided into two groups on each side of the area.

*Equipment.* Utility ball.

*Number of Players.* Six to twelve.

*Game.* Players stand one step in front of their own goal line. The players try to throw the ball over their opponents' goal line. The ball is thrown from the place where it is caught.

The ball must bounce at least once before crossing the opponents' goal line. One point is awarded each time the ball crosses the goal line.

*Teaching Suggestions.* Children with a weak throw may go to the center line to throw the ball. Advanced players may use two balls.

### Circle Pass

*Formation.* Single circle with the children facing the center of the circle.

*Equipment.* Utility ball.

*Number of Players.* Six to ten.

*Game.* The ball is passed across the circle using a chest pass or throw. All the players in the group count the number of passes their group can make in one minute. If a ball is missed, the count continues on the next throw.

Each time the game is played, try to improve the group's score.

*Teaching Suggestion.* Other types of passes may be used.

### Circuit Ball

*Formation.* Children equally distributed at each skill station.

*Equipment.* Six balls, a barrel or box, ten bowling pins, two wall targets, a floor maze, and an obstacle course.

*Number of Players.* Ten to fifteen.

*Game.* Each child is placed at a skill station in the gym. The children perform the skill at that station until the whistle is blown. At the whistle each child replaces the equipment and moves to the next station, where he performs the specified skill. Stations may change as new skills are taught.

A sample circuit might include the following:

1. Wall target for a short throw for speed.
2. A large wall target for a distance throw.
3. Barrel toss for accuracy.
4. Ten pins in a line for a rolling target.
5. Bouncing maze.
6. Dribble obstacle course.

*Teaching Suggestions.* A score card may be used for children who are able to understand and record scores. Also, adjust the circuit to the ability of the children.

## KICKING SKILLS

*Kicking a Stationary Ball.* Stand with the left foot to the side of the ball. The right leg is in back and up, with the toes pointing down. Swing the right leg downward and forward and contact the ball with the instep. Follow through forward after contact is made (Fig. 9-15).

*Kicking a Moving Ball.* The foot is placed near the ball as it hits the floor or at the desired contact point. Weight is placed on the left foot. The right leg makes contact with the ball right after the left foot is placed. Contact the ball with the instep and follow through (Fig. 9-16).

Figure 9-15                    Figure 9-16

*Dribbling.* Move right foot forward and push ball forward and slightly to the left, using the inside of the foot. Step on the right foot and repeat the action with the left foot, pushing the ball forward and slightly to the right. Keep the ball close. A skip step or short running steps between contacts helps to cover distance and maintain balance (Fig. 9-17).

*Punting.* The ball is held in both hands. The arms are extended and parallel to the ground. Step forward left, right, left. Bring the right leg forward as the ball is released. Extend the kicking leg and contact the ball on the top of the foot. Follow through upward (Fig. 9-18).

Figure 9-17                    Figure 9-18

## Kicking Skill Progression

The kicking skills listed below are in progressive order:

1. Kick a stationary ball.
2. Kick a stationary ball at a target.
3. Kick a stationary ball for distance.
4. Kick a moving ball.
5. Kick a moving ball at a target.
6. Kick a moving ball for distance.
7. Kick the ball with the inside of the foot.
8. Kick the ball with the outside of the foot.
9. Dribble the ball fifteen yards.
10. Punt a round ball.
11. Punt a football.

## Kicking Skill Games

### Target Kicking

*Formation.* One column behind the kicking line. Kicking line is twenty feet from target.

| 3 | 3 | blue |
|---|---|------|
| 2 | 2 | white |
| 1 | 1 | red |

Kicking Line

*Equipment.* Soccer or utility ball.

*Number of Players.* Four to six in each group.

*Game.* The first child in the column places the ball on the kicking line and kicks the stationary ball to the target. A ball hitting the red area is one point, the white area is two points, and the blue area is three points. Each child records his score on the blackboard.

Each child is given five kicks. The child with the highest total is the winner.

*Teaching Suggestion.* Increase the distance as the kicking skill of the children improves.

### Yard Club

*Formation.* Column formation behind the starting line.

| 25 yd. |
|--------|
| 20 yd. |
| 15 yd. |
| 10 yd. |
| kicking line |
| starting line |

*Equipment.* Utility or soccer balls.

*Number of Players.* Four to six in each group.

*Skill.* Kicking a stationary ball.

*Game.* The ball is given to one team on the fifteen-yard line. The ball is placed on the fifteen-yard line. One team member kicks the stationary ball. The opposing team catches the ball as close to their opponents' goal line as possible. The ball is placed on the ground at the point where it was caught. The new kicking team now attempts to kick the ball toward their opponents' goal. The point is declared when one team is forced to catch the ball behind the goal line which they are defending. The team with the most points at the end of the game period is the winner.

*Teaching Suggestions.* Give all children an opportunity to catch and kick the ball. If the game is slow, award the team five steps toward their opponents' goal line each time the ball is caught. Change the distance between goals to challenge participants.

## Kicking Games

*Note.* New skills not taught in ball handling would need to be taught before they are used in the games.

### One-Base Kick Ball

*Formation.* Children lined up behind home plate with several children in the field.

*Equipment.* One home plate, one base, one kick ball.

*Number of Players.* Six to twelve.

*Game.* Have all the children run from home plate to first base to establish the running path. Children who understand how to field the ball or the teacher's assistant will be the fielders. The teacher is the pitcher to begin.

The first player kicks a ball rolled by the pitcher and runs to first base, where he remains until the next player kicks the ball. The second player kicks the ball and runs to first base while the runner on first runs home. The player can be put out by touching the base with the ball or with the foot while in possession of the ball before the base runner reaches the base. After his turn at bat, each player goes to the end of the line at home base.

As the children become familiar with the procedure of the game, appoint the child who is put out to become the pitcher until the next runner is out. Then appoint the child who is put out to become the first baseman until the next runner is put out. He then progresses to be pitcher.

*Teaching Suggestions.* As the children learn the concept of playing fielder's position, change the game by adding fielders and play as a game of "work-up."

At first children will need to be reminded what they are to do when the ball is kicked. To help the children to determine the difference between being a base runner at first and the first baseman, teach the runner to crouch for a running start and the first baseman to put one foot on the base and reach toward the pitcher. This symbolism will help them to remember their responsibilities.

### Long-Base Kick Ball

*Formation.* One half of the children lined up behind home plate, with the other half of the children in the field.

*Equipment.* One home plate, one base, one kick ball.

*Number of Players.* Six to twelve.

*Game.* The first kicker kicks a ball rolled by the pitcher. The kicker runs around first base and home. The fielders attempt to get the kicker out by hitting him with the ball or throwing the ball to home plate before the kicker returns. All the players on the kicking team take their turn kicking the ball, then change with the team in the field. The team with the most runs wins. A run is a successful trip from home to first and back to home before the ball reaches home base or the kicker is hit with the ball.

*Teaching Suggestion.* The teacher may need to help the fielding team by being the catcher.

### Lineup Kick Ball

*Formation.* One half of the children lined up behind a restraining line drawn across the field at the point where second base would be. The rest of the children line up in the dugout behind home base.

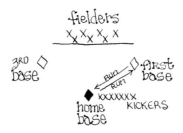

*Equipment.* One home plate, two bases, and a kick ball.

*Number of Players.* Six to twelve on each team.

*Game.* The children in the field should be spaced behind the restraining line in order to field any ball hit into the field between first and third bases. The first kicker kicks a stationary ball off home plate into the field and runs around first base and back to home plate. The player closest to the ball fields the ball and stands on the spot where he gains control of the ball while his teammates run and line up behind him.

If the fielding team should catch a fly ball or if their team lines up before the runner crosses home plate, the fielding team is awarded one point. If the kicker crosses home plate before the fielding team gets lined up, the kicking team is awarded one point. If a foul ball is kicked, the kicker may try again until he is able to kick a fair ball. After everyone on the kicking team has had a turn kicking the ball, the teams change places.

*Teaching Suggestions.* Traffic cones or bean bags may be used as substitutes for bases.

Encourage the children to line up behind the players in line rather than crowding into the line.

Only the player closest to the ball should field the ball. Running in front of another player to field the ball should be discouraged. The distance of the bases may be varied according to the player's ability.

### Danish Rounders

*Formation.* One half of the children line up behind a restraining line twenty-five to thirty feet from home base. The restraining line should be about eighty feet in length. The rest of the children line up in the dugout behind home plate.

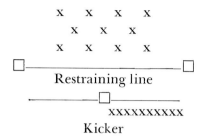

Equipment. One home plate, markers for the restraining line, and a kick ball.

*Number of Players.* Six to twelve on each team.

*Game.* The children in the field should be spaced behind the restraining line in order to field any ball hit into the field between the markers. The kicking team should be lined up to the right of home plate.

The first kicker kicks a stationary ball off home plate into the field and runs around his teammates.The kicking team counts loudly the number of times the runner is able to run completely around his team before the other team calls "Danish Rounders."

The player closest to the ball fields the ball and stands on the spot where he gains control of the ball while his teammates run and line up behind him. The fielder immediately begins passing the ball under his legs. Each fielder must receive and pass the ball until the last player on the team receives it. He runs with the ball to the front of the line and calls "Danish Rounders."

The kicking team receives one point for each time the kicker runs completely around his own team before "Danish Rounders" is called. If the fielding team catches a fly ball, the kicker is immediately out. If a foul ball is kicked, the kicker may try again until he is able to kick a fair ball. After everyone on the kicking team has had a turn kicking the ball, the teams change places.

*Teaching Suggestions.* See those for line-up kickball.

### Beat Ball

*Formation.* One half of the children line up in the dugout well behind home base. The other team assumes normal fielding positions for softball or kick ball.

*Equipment.* Three bases, a home plate, and a kick ball.

*Number of Players.* Eight to twelve on each team.

*Game.* The pitcher rolls the ball to the first kicker, who kicks it into the field. The kicker runs around the outside of the bases until he crosses home plate. The fielder closest to the kicked ball fields the ball and throws it to first base.

The first baseman catches the ball and touches first base while in possession of the ball, and then throws the ball to second base. The second and third baseman receive the ball and proceed as the first baseman did. The catcher at home base receives the ball and touches home plate.

If the catcher touches home base while in possession of the ball before the runner crosses home base, the runner is out. If the runner crosses home base before the catcher touches home base with the ball, the kicking team receives one point. If the fielding team catches a fly ball, the kicker is out. If the kicker kicks a foul ball, he may try again until he is able to kick a fair ball. The kicker may not cross home base before the ball is kicked.

After everyone on the kicking team has had a turn kicking the ball, the teams change places.

*Teaching Suggestions.* The pitcher should roll the ball, not bounce it.

Encourage the basemen to play on the inside corner of their bases so the runner will not interfere with the ball while running around the bases.

Rotate the players so all children have a turn playing bases.

### Stunt Ball

*Formation.* Same formation as that used for beat ball or softball.

*Equipment.* Three bases, a kick ball, two basketballs, two bowling pins, and two short jump ropes.

*Number of Players.* Eight to twelve on each team.

*Game.* The game is played like beat Ball with the exception that at each base the runner and the baseman must perform either a skill or a novelty stunt.

After kicking the ball fairly into the field, the kicker runs around the bases, stopping long enough to perform a stunt at each base. The fielders must throw the ball to first, second, third, and home, in that order. Upon receiving the ball each baseman must also perform the stunt and touch the base before throwing the ball to the next base.

A run is scored if (a) the runner reaches home plate before the ball or (b) an opponent interferes with the runner while he is running the bases or performing a stunt. A runner is out if (a) the ball reaches home first, (b) a fly ball is caught, or (c) a runner interferes with the fielding of a ball or the completing of a stunt. If the kicker kicks a foul ball, he may try again until he is able to kick a fair ball. The kicker may not cross home base before the ball is kicked.

After everyone on the kicking team has had a turn kicking the ball, the teams change places.

Possible stunts may be jump-the-rope three times, five jumping jacks, a forward roll, Indian sit-down, make a basket, knock down a bowling pin and reset it using the feet, jump-the-rope backwards, three push-ups, or stunts from the stunts unit.

*Teaching Suggestions.* Change basemen often.

Wastebaskets may be used for baskets.

All stunts should be done correctly; if they are done incorrectly, they should be repeated.

### Kick Ball

*Formation.* Assume fielding positions used for softball for one team. The other team should line up in the dugout in a safe area behind home base.

*Equipment.* Three bases, a home plate, a kickball, and a pitcher's plate.

*Number of Players.* Eight to twelve on each team.

*Game.* The rules are the same as for softball, with a few exceptions: (a) the pitcher rolls the ball, and (b) the kicker kicks the ball to put the ball into play. Also, the kicker may not cross home base before the ball is kicked, and, when a soft playground ball is used, the runner may be put out if he is hit below the waist by the ball.

*Teaching Suggestions.* The pitcher should roll the ball, not bounce it.

Encourage the basemen to play off the base to field balls, and to play the inside of the base to make a forced out or tag out. This provides for better play and causes less interference.

Rotate the players so all children have a turn playing the bases.

## Soccer Games

### Boundary Ball

*Formation.* Each team assumes a scattered formation on one half of the playing area.

*Equipment.* One soccer or playground ball.

*Number of Players.* Ten to fifteen on each team.

*Game.* The goal line is the end line of each team's playing area. The ball is placed in the center of the playing area. One member of each team places one foot on the ball. With the signal to begin, the two players try to pull the ball to their side of the floor. The players on both teams move about in their half of the floor attempting to kick the ball through the opposing team and over their goal line and at the same time prevent the ball from crossing the goal line on their half of the floor. The players may not touch the ball with their hands.

A goal is scored each time the ball crosses the opposing team's goal line. Each goal is one point.

*Teaching Suggestions.* To prevent leaving an unguarded space and to allow room to play the ball, encourage the players to play areas on the floor rather than grouping around the ball. The size of the area may be adjusted to provide for more or less play according to the ability and number of the players. For children more advanced in their ability to play, two balls may be used.

### Circle Soccer

*Formation.* Each team forms one half of the circle, with approximately two feet between players.

*Equipment.* One soccer or playground ball.

*Number of Players.* Eight to ten on each team.

*Game.* The ball is awarded to one team on the edge of the circle. The team with the ball kicks it toward the opponents, attempting to kick the ball past the opponents through the circle. The defending team attempts to prevent the ball from going outside the circle by blocking and trapping the ball.

Before kicking the ball across the circle, the attacking team must control the ball by stopping it. If a player uses his hands on the ball, the opposing team is awarded a point. If the ball is kicked over the shoulders of the defending team, a point is awarded the defending team. Each goal is worth one point.

*Teaching Suggestions.* When kicking the ball, encourage the players to use deception rather than power. For deception, encourage the players to use the inside and outside of the foot.

### Team Circle Soccer

*Formation.* Each team forms one half of the circle, with approximately two feet between players.

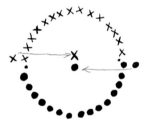

*Equipment.* One soccer or playground ball.

*Number of Players.* Eight to fifteen on each team.

*Game.* One player from each team moves to the center of the circle from opposite sides of the circle. The ball is placed in the center of the circle. Then two players in the center of the circle place one foot on the ball while facing the opposing team. With the signal to begin, the two players try to pull the ball free and control the ball. The two center players attempt to keep the ball away from each other by dribbling inside the circle until they can deceptively kick the ball past the opponents through the circle for a goal. Each goal counts one point.

The players on the edge of the circle attempt to prevent the ball from going outside the circle by blocking and trapping the ball. These players should control the ball and pass it strategically to their teammate in the center of the circle. When a teammate on the edge of the circle has the ball, the circle player should move to an open area to receive a pass, dribble, and try to score.

Using the hands on the ball is illegal. Kicking the ball too hard is dangerous kicking and is a foul. Kicking the ball higher than the shoulders is also a foul. For all fouls, the opposing team is given a free kick in the center of the circle by the circle player with the opposing circle player at least five yards away. It is also illegal for an opposing player to step between a player who is about to play the ball and the ball. This foul is called obstruction.

After a point has been scored or a time limit called, the players in the center of the circle exit on the oppoiste side of the circle from which they came onto the floor and all players rotate one position in the circle.

*Teaching Suggestions.* When kicking the ball, the players should use deception rather than power.

When a teammate on the edge of the circle has the ball, the circle players should move away from the ball to get free for a pass.

In this game players should use passing, dribbling, dodging, and trapping rather than kicking.

When the number of players is sufficient, one player from each team may be assigned to officiate the game. The players rotate in and out of the officiating position in the same manner the players rotate in and out of the center of the circle.

## Bombardment

*Formation.* A rectangle with each team lined up lengthwise on the outside of the area. Eight markers are placed in alternating colors on a line in the center of the area.

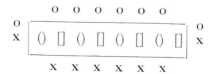

*Equipment.* A soccer ball or a playground ball and eight markers (traffic cones or liquid containers which tip easily), four of one color and four of another color.

*Number of Players.* Eight to fifteen on each team.

*Game.* Space the players along the kicking line with one player from each team on the sideline. The ball is awarded to one team on the kicking line. The player by the ball attempts to kick the ball from behind his kicking line and knock down one of his team's markers. The ball should be trapped by the receiving team by the player closest to the ball and kicked at one of his team's markers. If a player should knock down one of his opponents' markers, the marker stays down and counts as a score for that team.

The sideline players try to prevent the ball from going over the sideline, and kick the ball to their own team behind the kicking line. They may also recover any ball which stops in their quarter of the rectangle.

Using the hands on the ball, dangerous kicking, and stepping over the kicking line are fouls. The penalty for a foul is to award the ball to the opposing team and cancel any score made on that play. Sideline players may not attempt to knock down the center markers.

*Teaching Suggestions.* Rotate the players after each point or after a predetermined time limit. Also, encourage the players to trap the ball before kicking it at a marker.


### Line Soccer

*Formation.* A rectangle with each team lined up on three sides of the court.

|            | o | o | o | x | x | x |            |
|------------|---|---|---|---|---|---|------------|
| Goal Line  | o |   | o | x |   | x | Goal Line  |
|            | o |   | o | x |   | x |            |
|            | o |   | o | x |   | x |            |
|            | o | o | o | x | x | x |            |

*Equipment.* One soccer or playground ball and two sets of colored pinnies to distinguish the teams.

*Number of Players.* Twelve to sixteen on each team.

*Game.* Each team should space three or four players on the end line, each sideline, and behind the center line, which divided the rectangle in half. The players on the end line are defensive players who protect the goal line, which is the end line. The players on the two sidelines prevent the ball from going over the sideline and pass the ball to the active players on the floor.

The game is started with the players in the center of the floor, spaced on their half of the floor behind the center line. The ball is placed in the center of the rectangle. Two opposing players place one foot on the ball while facing the opposing team. With the signal to begin, the two players try to pull the ball free and pass it to a teammate. The players in the center of the floor may move within the rectangle to help defend their goal and to attempt to control the ball by passing and dribbling until they can score by kicking the ball through the opposing defensive players and over the opponent's goal line. Each goal counts one point.

Using the hands on the ball, dangerous kicking, kicking the ball over the goal line above the shoulders, obstruction, kicking other players, and pushing are fouls. The penalty for a foul is to award the ball to the opposing team for a free kick on the spot where the foul occurred or five yards away from the goal line. No players may be within five yards of the free kick.

After a goal has been scored or a time limit elapsed, rotate each set of three or four players to the next assignment on the floor.

*Teaching Suggestions.* Encourage the players to use teamwork and play areas of the floor instead of grouping near the ball. The active players should move to an open area to receive a pass rather than crowd around the ball. Also, the players should try to control the ball instead of kicking it from one end of the area to the other end.

## Forwards and Backs

*Formation.* A rectangle with a center line across the middle of the area.

```
          X                          O
              O    O   X     X
          X        X           O     O
Goal Line          O    O   X     X          Goal Line
          X        X           O     O
              O    O   X     X
          X                          O
```

*Equipment.* One soccer ball or playground ball and two sets of colored pinnies to distinguish the teams.

*Number of Players.* Twelve to sixteen on each team.

*Game.* Each team should designate half of their players as forwards and half of their players as backs. The backs stay on their team's half of the area, defend their goal line, which is the end line of the rectangle, and pass the ball over the center line to their forwards. The forwards stay in their opponents' half of the rectangle and attempt to score by kicking the ball over the opponents' goal line.

The game is started with the ball on the center line. Two opposing forwards place one foot on the ball while facing their defensive players. On the signal to begin, the two players try to pull the ball to their half of the floor and pass it to a teammate.

The players should be assigned general areas on the field to play. This will help them cover the area and provide for more passing room.

Using the hands on the ball, dangerous kicking, kicking the ball over the goal line above the shoulders, obstruction, kicking other players, pushing, and crossing the center line are fouls. The penalty for a foul is to award the ball to the opposing team for a free kick on the spot where the foul occurred or five yards away from the goal line. No players may be within five yards of the free kick. The kicker may not play the ball until it has been played by another player.

Each goal counts one point. After the goal, the team scored against is given possession of the ball on the center line.

If the ball is kicked out of bounds, the ball is awarded to the opposing team for a throw-in with everyone five yards away.

*Teaching Suggestions.* First, the players should try to control the ball and get free for passes rather than crowding around the ball. Secondly, at the halfway point in the game, the players should change positions on the team.

### Soccer

Children who are able to play the lead-up games presented previously are ready to play soccer, which is an excellent, exciting, and vigorous game. The rules are available in *Soccer Guides* for girls or boys. Most of the basic rules have been incorporated in the lead-up games presented previously. The following are some variations:

*Scooter Soccer.* Regular soccer rules are used with the addition that all participants must play the game on gym scooters.

*Crab Soccer.* Regular soccer rules are used with the exception that all players assume a crab walk position to play the game.

### FOOTBALL

*Passing.* Stand with the left foot forward. The ball is held toward the end of the ball with the fingers on the laces of the ball and the thumb on the opposite side of the ball. Move the ball up and back behind the ear, with the shoulder and body rotated away from the target. Rotate the body toward the target and whip the arm forward with the elbow leading, snap the wrist forward, and release the ball off the fingers as the hand draws under the ball. Step into the throw and keep the nose of the ball slightly up (Fig. 9-19).

*Centering.* Assume a wide stride position and bend down and forward into a crouch position with the hands on the ball, which is slightly in front of the head and shoulders. Grip the ball in the same manner used for a forward pass (Fig. 9-20).

*Handoff.* To receive the ball, hold the forearms parallel to the ground in front of the body with the palms toward each other and ball-width apart. Lean slightly forward. The ball is placed firmly into the midsection of the receiver by the player with the ball. The receiver holds the ball with both hands. To carry the ball the receiver pulls the ball to the side, away from the oppon-

Figure 9-19                              Figure 9-20

ent, and carries it tucked against the elbow and body with the hand over the nose of the ball.

## Football Games

### *Punt and Run*

*Formation.* Children in a scatter formation with the kicker facing the group.

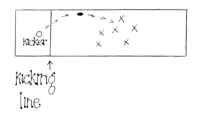

*Equipment.* One football.
*Number of Players.* Six to ten.

*Game.* The kicker punts the ball toward the group. The player closest to the ball catches the ball and runs to the kicking line. The kicker runs to the catching area with the other children. The process is repeated with the new kicker.

*Teaching Suggestions.* Encourage the children to carry the ball correctly. Also, provide for all children to have a turn catching the ball.

For children with some experience, a variation may be added in which the kicker tries to touch the ball carrier with a two-hand touch below the waist. If he is successful, he remains in the kicking position.

### Punt Back

*Formation.* Two teams face each other on the field, kicking-distance apart.

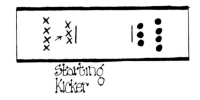

*Equipment.* One football.

*Number of Players.* Six to eight on each team.

*Game.* Each group stands on one half of the field. The kicker on one of the teams kicks the ball from the middle of their half of the field or what would be the twenty-five-yard line on a football field. The player on the other team closest to the ball attempts to catch the ball. If he is successful, he may take five giant steps toward the opponents' goal line. If the ball bounces, it must be kicked from the spot where the player gained control of it. The process is repeated, with each team trying to force the opposing team backward until they fail to gain control of the ball before it crosses their goal line. When a team fails to gain control of the ball before it crosses their goal line, a touchdown is scored. Each touchdown counts six points.

*Teaching Suggestions.* Provide for all children to have a turn catching the ball. The best catching technique is to trap the ball against the body and give as the ball is caught.

### Field Ball

*Formation.* Two teams, one on each half of the field.

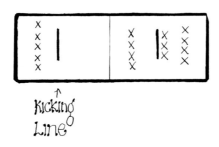

Equipment. One football.

Number of Players. Eight to ten on each team.

*Game.* The receiving team scatters on their half of the field to receive the kick from the opposing team. The kicking team may not cross the center line until the receiving team has gained control of the ball. The receiving team may advance the ball by passing in any direction or running with the ball. Any number of passes is permissible.

The defensive team must tag the ball carrier with a two-hand touch below the waist. There is no body contact in the game other than the touch. When the defensive team makes the touch, they become the offensive team and have one down to move the ball. The offensive team has one down to score a touchdown, which counts six points. An intercepted pass and the return of the kickoff do not count as downs. A ball kicked out of bounds on the kickoff is kicked again.

Holding, blocking, pushing, and tripping are illegal. If the defensive team fouls, the ball is moved forward eight paces from the spot of the foul. If the offensive team fouls, the defensive team is awarded the ball at the spot of the foul. The ball may not be placed closer than five yards to the goal. The ball is dead when it touches the ground.

*Teaching Suggestions.* For experienced players, the game may be restricted to only one forward pass and lateral passes. The size of the field also should be adjusted to the ability of the players.

### Seven-Man Touch Football

*Formation.* Two teams, one on each half of a football field.

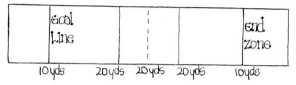

*Equipment.* One football.

*Number of Players.* Seven on each team: left end, center, right end, quarterback, fullback, right halfback, and left halfback.

*Game.* This game is played and scored in the same manner as regular football, with the modifications as listed.

If the kickoff goes out of bounds, the kicking team is given another chance to kick. If this happens a second time, the receiving team puts the ball in play at the fifty-yard line. On all plays the ball is placed at least five yards from the sideline.

When a player with the ball is touched with two hands below the waist by an opponent, the play stops. If the ball is fumbled, the play stops and the team which last had possession puts the ball in play at the spot where the ball hit the ground.

The offensive team has four downs to advance the ball to the next zone on the field or to score a touchdown. A new series of downs is started when a team crosses a zone line.

The offensive team must have three players on the scrimmage line to begin each play.

Any player except the center is an eligible pass receiver.

Body contact is illegal. The only form of blocking which may be used is to place the body in the way of an opponent. Neither team may use the hands when blocking. Both feet must be on the ground. The penalty for infraction of the rules is to award five yards to the nonoffending team. For unnecessary roughness or unsportsmanlike conduct, fifteen yards is awarded. The penalty for pass interference is to rule the pass completed. For situations not mentioned apply regulation football rules.

*Teaching Suggestions.* Rotate players in the position. Also, adjust the time limit and size of the field to the ability of the players.

Nine-man touch football may be played with the same rules, by adding two linemen. In eleven-man touch football each team has two guards and two tackles in addition to the players used for seven-man touch football.

Flag football may be played with the same rules by using a flag tucked in the belt of each player. When the flag is removed the ball carrier is stopped.

## HITTING SKILLS

*Two-Hand Underhand Hit or Volley.* Stand with the body bent slightly forward, the knees flexed, and the arms straight forward. The hands are open, with one hand clasped inside the other. One foot is slightly in front of the other. Contact underside of the ball on the forearms and let the ball bounce upward and outward toward the direction intended (Fig. 9-21).

Figure 9-21                    Figure 9-22

*One-Hand Underhand Hit.* The ball is held in front of the right side by the left hand. The left foot is forward. Weight is on the right foot and the right arm is back, ready to hit. Transfer the weight forward to the left foot as the right arm swings forward. Contact the ball off the left hand with the heel of the hand near the bottom of the ball. Follow through in the direction of the ball (Fig. 9-22). This technique may be used to hit a low ball by reaching under the ball and letting it rebound off the arm and hand.

*One-Hand Side Hit.* Stand with the left side toward the direction of the target. Hold the ball in the left hand in front of the left leg. The right arm moves backward and forward simultaneously with a weight transfer in the same direction. Contact the ball with the heel of the hand behind and slightly under the ball (Fig. 9-23).

Figure 9-23

*Overhand Hit or Volley.* Bend the knees. The elbows are bent and in a sideward poistion. The fingers are spread and curved, with the thumbs and forefingers together and the palms upward. Contact the ball above the head and extend the fingers, arms, and body upward. Complete the follow-through in the intended direction of the hit. Hit from a stationary position under the ball, facing the intended direction of the ball (Fig. 9-24).

Figure 9-24

## Hitting Skill Progression

The following are underhand hitting skills:

1. Bounce the ball then hit it upward.
2. Hit a ball tossed from a partner.
3. Hit a bounced ball to a partner who will hit it after it bounces.
4. With a partner, consecutively hit the ball allowing only one bounce between hits.
5. Throw the ball against the wall and hit the return with an underhand hit.
6. Count consecutive underhand hits with a partner—no bounces allowed.
7. While volleying with a partner, hit the ball so it lands in a large circle.
8. Play "Two Square," as described in the next section.

9. Play "Four Square," described in the next section.

Sidearm hitting skills are as follows:

1. Hit for distance.
2. Hit over a net at variable heights.
3. Play tetherball.

Overhand hitting skills are listed below:

1. Toss the ball in the air and catch it in the proper overhand hitting position.
2. Toss the ball in the air and hit the ball upward.
3. Toss the ball several feet away, move under the ball, and catch it in the right position.
4. Toss the ball several feet away, get under the ball, and hit the ball upward.
5. Hit a ball tossed by a partner.
6. Throw the ball against the wall and hit the rebound with an overhand hit.
7. Volley with a group in a circle, hitting the ball high.
8. Volley the ball with a partner.

### Hitting Skill Games

*Two Square*

*Formation.* One child in each square.

*Equipment.* One utility ball for each two children.

*Number of Players.* Two for each game maze.

*Game.* Each child stands just inside the end line of one square. One player serves the ball by bouncing the ball and hitting it underhand into the opposite square. If the opposing player fails to return the ball with an underhand hit, the serving player gets a point. After the service, the ball continues in play until one player fails to return the ball to the opposite square. If the serving player fails to return the ball, the opponent is awarded one point and the service. Play continues until one player gains fifteen points. Note: The ball must be hit upward.

*Teaching Suggestions.* To simplify the game, have the receiver catch the service and return the ball with a serve. The player gains a point when his opponent fails to catch the ball after one bounce or fails to hit it so it lands in the opposite square.

For more advanced players, designate the squares A and B. The objective is to stay in square A. If the player in square A makes an error, the player in square B rotates to square A.

More players can play by having a new player rotate in each time a player in one of the squares commits an error. This is sometimes difficult to play with children who have a short attention span.

**Four Square**

*Formation.* One child in each square.

*Equipment.* One utility ball for each four players.

*Number of Players.* Four for each game maze.

*Game.* Player D serves the ball by bouncing the ball and hitting it from behind the serving line into any one of the other three squares. The player in the square into which the ball was served must return the ball after it has bounced once.

Play continues until a foul is committed. The player committing the foul moves to square D and everyone below him moves one square toward A.

The ball must be hit upward so it lands within an opponent's square. Other fouls consist of causing the ball to touch a line, contacting the ball with any part of the body other than the hands and forearms, holding or throwing the ball, not returning the ball after one bounce, hitting the ball with the closed fist, and causing the ball to go out of bounds.

*Teaching Suggestion.* The teaching suggestions for "Two Square" may also apply to "Four Square."

**Volley Handball**

*Formation.* Two players facing the wall.

*Equipment.* One utility ball for each two players.

*Number of Players.* Two in each game.

*Game.* One player serves the ball by bouncing the ball and

hitting it against the wall above the three-foot line. The second player must hit the ball after one bounce. Play continues until one player fails to return the ball above the three-foot line. Players alternate hits.

A player scores a point each time his opponent makes an error. The service alternates. The first player to score fifteen points wins the game.

*Teaching Suggestions.* A hit which purposely causes the ball to hit near the base of the wall is illegal. Also, more players can play by having a new player rotate in each time a player commits an error.

### Tetherball

*Formation.* Tetherball court.

*Equipment.* Tetherball rope seven and a half feet long and a pole ten feet long with a line five feet from the ground.

*Number of Players.* Two.

*Game.* One player stands in each half of the circle. One player starts the game by throwing the ball into the air and hitting it with the hand or fist in the direction he chooses. The opposing player must let the ball pass him once. He must hit the ball in the opposite direction on the second swing around the pole. The player who winds the ball around the pole above the five-foot line is the winner.

*Teaching Suggestions.* A third child may hold the ball so that the rope is taut for the service.

Gradually add more rules to include other fouls in the game. The additional fouls are throwing the ball, touching the ball with any part of the body other than hands, touching the pole hitting the rope, and playing the ball while outside the playing area.

### Beginning Handball

*Formation.* Players stand behind the service line.

*Equipment.* Sponge-rubber ball, volleyball, or utility ball; handball court.

*Number of Players.* Two to four.

*Game.* Player No. 1 serves the ball by batting it against the ground, causing the ball to rebound against the wall and back into the playing area. Player No. 2 returns the ball by batting the ball after one bounce so that it again rebounds from the wall.

Play continues until a player misses the ball or causes it to go out of bounds. The player who does not commit the error is given one point. The serve alternates. The first player to gain fifteen points wins the game.

*Teaching Suggestions.* More bounces may be allowed for the beginner. Also, additional players may be included in the game by rotating them in for the player committing the error.

### Handball

*Formation.* Players stand behind the service line, which is fifteen feet from the wall.

*Equipment.* Sponge-rubber ball, volleyball, utility ball, or tennis ball; handball court.

*Number of Players.* Two to four players.

*Game.* Player No. 1 serves the ball by letting it bounce on the floor and then hitting it against the wall so it rebounds back into the playing area. Player No. 2 returns the ball by hitting the ball after one bounce or before the bounce so the ball will rebound from the wall into the playing area.

Play continues until a player misses the ball or fails to cause it to hit the wall. The player who does not commit the error is given one point. The serve alternates. The first player to gain fifteen points wins the game.

*Teaching Suggestions.* More bounces may be allowed for the beginner. Also, additional players may be included in the game by rotating them in for the player committing the error.

*Variations.* Two-wall handball or three-wall handball can be played to add skill to the game. The ball may be hit at an angle such that the ball will rebound off the side wall, hit the front wall, and rebound into the playing area. The ball must hit the front wall last to be a legal hit. The other rules are the same as handball.

## Paddle Tennis

Paddle tennis is played like tennis with the exception that on the serve the ball is hit after it has been dropped and bounced once. Short paddles or "shorty" tennis rackets are used to simplify the skill.

## Bounce Keep-It-Up

*Formation.* Single circle with the players facing the center of the circle.

*Equipment.* Utility ball or volleyball.

*Number of Players.* Six to eight in each group.

*Game.* One player in each group tosses the ball up to himself and volleys the ball upward and toward another circle player. Players continue to volley the ball into the air and the entire group calls the number of each consecutive hit. The ball must bounce once between each hit. Also, the ball must be contacted with the hands or forearms only, and be clearly batted. Each group attempts to improve the number of consecutive hits without a miss.

*Teaching Suggestions.* A more advanced variation would be to try to volley the ball without a bounce. If the ball is missed, the ball is in play after one bounce. If the ball is hit successfully after one bounce, the counting continues.

## Bounce Net Ball

*Formation.* Children in two lines facing the net.

*Equipment.* One volleyball or utility ball for each group, nets five to six feet high.

*Number of Players.* Two to six in each group.

*Game.* One player begins by bouncing the ball and hitting it over the net. Player on the opposite side returns the ball after it bounces. The ball may be played as long as it remains in bounds and keeps bouncing.

The ball must be batted and not caught or thrown. When an error is committed the opposing team is given the serve and one point. The first team to get fifteen points wins.

*Teaching Suggestions.* As the skill of the group improves, (a) limit the number of bounces to one, (b) increase the height of the net, and (c) start the service near the middle of the court and gradually move it back. Also, a regular underhand serve without a bounce can be substituted when the skill of the players is appropriate.

The teacher or another skilled player on each side will help the game to progress and control the practice of the group.

### Catch Volleyball

*Formation.* One team on each side of the net in a scattered formation.

*Equipment.* Volleyball, net about six feet high, and a volleyball court.

*Number of Players.* Ten to twelve.

*Game.* One player hits the ball over the net. Any player on the opposite team attempts to catch the ball. A player who catches the ball must hit it back over the net. One point is awarded the serving team if the receiving team does not catch the ball. One point is awarded the receiving team if they catch the ball before it bounces. The first team to get fifteen points wins the game.

*Teaching Suggestions.* Use an underhand serve to hit the ball at first. As skill improves, have each child toss the ball to himself and volley it over the net.

## Lead-up Games to Volleyball

### One-Bounce Volleyball

*Formation.* One team on each side of the net in a regular volleyball position.

*Equipment.* Volleyball, net about three feet high, and a volleyball court.

*Number of Players.* Six to eight on each court.

*Game.* The right back player on the serving team, using an underhand serve, hits the ball over the net to the opposing team. The ball must bounce once and only once before it is returned across the net. Each team may have three hits to return the ball over the net. The ball may be hit only once in succession by any one player.

The game is scored in the same manner as regulation volleyball.

*Teaching Suggestions.* The team will have better success in returning the ball over the net if the serve is hit before it bounces on the receiving team's side of the court.

The players should be taught to hit the ball cleanly. Also, this game serves as a good opportunity to learn to hit the ball without having to make a powerful hit.

### Newcomb

*Formation.* One team on each side of the net in regular volleyball positions.

*Equipment.* Volleyball, a volleyball court, and a net at the appropriate height for the children's ability.

*Number of Players.* Six to eight on each team.

*Game.* The right back player serves the ball by throwing it over the net. Players on the opposite team catch the ball and may either pass it to a teammate or throw it over the net. The player who has possession of the ball may take only one step before releasing the ball. The object of the game is to place the ball between players of the opposing team so they cannot catch it and return the ball.

The game is scored in the same manner as regular volleyball. Only the serving team may score points. When either team fails to catch the ball or causes the ball to go out of bounds, either a point or side-out is called.

*Teaching Suggestions.* This game provides a good opportunity to teach scoring procedures and strategy of regular volleyball.

The players should keep the ball moving quickly to catch the opponent off guard.

### Keep-It-Up

*Formation.* Circle on each side of the volleyball court.

*Equipment.* A volleyball or playground ball.

*Number of Players.* Six to eight in each circle.

*Game.* On the signal to begin, one player in each circle tosses the ball to himself and hits it to another member of the circle. The players continue to hit the ball *up* and toward other players in the circle. The group calls the number of each consecutive hit until an illegal hit is made or the ball lands on the floor. The objective is to hit the ball as many consecutive hits as possible without letting the ball hit the floor. The group with the most consecutive hits in the alloted time period wins the game.

No one may play the ball twice in succession. The ball may not rest momentarily on the hands of a player. The ball may not touch the body below the waist.

*Teaching Suggestions.* Encourage the players to clearly bat the ball to call their own illegal hits. For less skilled players, one bounce may be allowed in order to keep the ball in play longer.

Remind the players to hit the ball high to allow time for a teammate to move under the ball. Moving into the proper hitting position is very important in order to play the ball correctly.

*Variations.* Two players may play the game, or the game may be played by an individual player against the wall. A line drawn on the wall will help the players to hit the ball with more control and consistency.

### Balloon Volleyball

Using the same procedure as for regular volleyball, use a large balloon instead of a volleyball. There is no limit on the number of hits.

### Cage Ball

*Formation.* Scatter formation on a regular volleyball court.

*Equipment.* A cage ball and a sturdy net at volleyball height.

*Number of Players.* Six to twenty on a team.

*Game.* The player in the right back position throws the ball into the air. The other players on his team may assist in hitting the ball over the net with no limit on the number of hits.

The game is played like volleyball with no limit on the number of hits. If the ball is allowed to hit the floor a point or side-out is called.

*Teaching Suggestions.* Players should be encouraged to play areas of the court rather than follow the ball. This will provide for more play.

This game will help the players get over any fear of hitting smaller balls. Less skill is needed to play this game; therefore, more players may play the game with success.

### Modified Volleyball

*Formation.* Regulation volleyball positions on the court.

*Equipment.* A volleyball and a net at appropriate height for the skill of the players.

*Number of Players.* Six to nine on each court.

*Game.* The game is played in the same manner as regulation volleyball with the possible modifications listed below, which may be used according to the ability of the players. (Fig. 9-25).

Figure 9-25

Allow two serves or an assist on the serve to get the ball in play. Move the serving distance up to accommodate the ability of the players. Allow as many hits on a side as necessary for enough play to keep interest in the game. Modified rules allow for one player to hit the ball twice in succession and three people to hit the ball before it crosses over the net.

*Teaching Suggestions.* Use more players on the court to cover the space, but not so many that there is not an opportunity to hit the ball frequently. Provide for automatic rotation so no player stays out of the game longer than for one point. Allow for one bounce to keep the ball in play.

Encourage the players to use a bounce pass for balls at chest level and below. The ball should be hit high to a teammate and low to the opposing team. Stress team play by encouraging passes to teammates.

The players should maintain a good ready position and slide to move under the ball to play correctly.

### BATTING SKILLS

Stand with the left side toward the pitcher. Spread the legs comfortably. Grip the bat with the left hand near the end of the bat and the right hand touching the left hand. Elbows are bent and away from the body, and the weight is evenly distributed (Fig. 9-26). Swing the bat parallel to the ground. Keep the eyes on the ball. As the bat swings forward, push on rear leg for more

Figure 9-26

power. Follow through with the bat, swinging around the left side as the weight transfers to the left foot.

## Batting Skill Progression

This list is ordered progressively:
1. Hit a stationary ball off a batting tee (Fig. 9-27).
2. Hit a ball pitched underhand (Fig. 9-28).
3. Hit a ball pitched overhand.
4. Fungo hitting.

Figure 9-27               Figure 9-28

## Softball Skill Games

### *Five Pitches*

*Formation.* Participants stand with both feet touching a line which is pitching-distance away from the target.

*Equipment.* One softball for every two children, and a wall target eighteen inches wide and thirty-two inches high, with the lower edge sixteen inches from the floor.

*Number of Players.* Two for each target.

*Game.* One player stands on a line pitching-distance away from the target. He throws the ball with an underhand pitch at the target on the wall. Each player is given five pitches at the target. One point is given for each ball which lands in the strike zone or target.

The second player stands near the target and returns the ball to the pitcher. After five pitches the participants change positions.

*Teaching Suggestion.* Encourage the participants to use proper pitching form and rules.

### Hoop Ball

*Formation.* Player No. 1 stands thirty feet away from the wall while Player No. 2 stands near the wall to retrieve the ball.

*Equipment.* One softball for each target. The target is a hula hoop taped to the wall, with the lower edge two feet away from the floor.

*Number of Players.* Two for each target.

*Game.* Player No. 1 throws the ball with an overhand throw at the hoop. He must stay behind the throwing line, which is thirty feet away from the target. Each player is given five throws at the hoop. One point is given for each ball which lands in the hoop.

Player No. 2 retrieves the ball and throws it back to player No. 1. After five pitches the players change positions. The player with the highest total after a designated number of throws is the winner.

*Teaching Suggestions.* Vary the throwing distance according to the skill of the participants. Designate the number of throws according to the ability of the children to tally scores.

### Goal-Line Softball

*Formation.* Two teams lined up in front of their goal line.

*Equipment.* One softball.

*Number of Players.* Ten to twelve.

*Game.* A player on one team must throw the ball from behind the throwing line. He attempts to throw the ball over the opponents' goal line. The ball must bounce at least once before crossing the goal. The receiving team catches the ball before it crosses the goal line; the player who catches the ball throws it from where it is caught.

One point is earned each time the ball is thrown over the goal of an opponent. The team with the highest total points wins.

*Teaching Suggestions.* Larger balls may be used for less-skilled players. Provide an opportunity for all children to throw the ball.

### One Base

*Formation.* Two batters, a catcher, one baseman, and several fielders.

*Equipment.* One base, one home plate, and one softball.

*Number of Players.* Nine to twelve.

```
              x

     x        x  □x
              x
              □
              x
```

*Game.* Player No. 1 throws the ball into the field and tries to run to the base and back home. The fielders field the ball and try to get the ball to the catcher before the runner reaches home. If the runner reaches home before the ball, he scores a run. If the ball reaches home before the runner, the runner is out. The runner then takes a fielder's position and the catcher becomes a batter. The fielders are numbered or named and work up to become the catcher. The player with the most runs is the winner.

*Teaching Suggestion.* For more advanced players, the runner may stop at the base and return home on the next turn.

### Softball Beat Ball

*Formation.* One team in the field, the other at bat.

*Equipment.* Three bases, one home plate, and one softball.

*Number of Players.* Six to eighteen

*Game.* The catchers throw the ball to first as the runner leaves home base. The basemen try to relay the ball around the bases before the runner completes his circuit around the bases. Each baseman must touch the base while in possession of the ball. The baserunner must touch each base while making the circuit.

If the baserunner reaches home plate before the ball, a run is scored. If the ball reaches home plate before the runner, the runner is out. Three outs and the teams change places.

*Teaching Suggestions.* With a small number of players, the game can be played with "work-up" rules (see below).

Adjust the distance of the bases to the ability of the players. Also, change the number of times around the bases for the runners and the throwers according to the skill of the group.

### Under the Leg

Play regular softball rules with the exception that the ball is thrown under one leg by the batter rather than using a bat. The batter must catch the ball thrown by the pitcher before throwing the ball into the field. If the batter fails to catch the ball which is in the strike zone, he is out.

### Five Hits

*Formation.* One player at bat, one catcher, and fielders.

*Equipment.* One softball diamond, a batting tee, and one softball.

*Number of Players.* Four to twelve.

*Game.* The batter hits the ball off the batting tee. A ball landing in the infield scores one point. A ball landing in the outfield scores two points.

Each batter hits five balls. His score is the total points gained after five hits. After hitting the ball five times the batter changes positions with a fielder.

*Teaching Suggestions.* Use a batting tee until the children can use fungo hitting. Also, point value can be changed when the participants understand larger numbers.

## Lead-up Games

### Hit the Bat

*Formation.* Group of children facing a batter.

```
                              xxxx
             x                xxxxx
                              xxxx
```

*Equipment.* One bat and two softballs.

*Number of Players.* Six to ten in a group.

*Game.* The batter, using "fungo" hits, sends the ball into the field toward the remainder of the players. The fielder closest to the ball fields the ball. If the ball is caught on the fly, the fielder becomes the batter. If the ball bounces two times, the fielder becomes the batter. If the fielder can roll the ball from the spot where he gained control of the ball and hit the bat placed on the ground in front of the batter, the fielder becomes the batter.

*Teaching Suggestions.* Children should not run in front of other children to field the ball. Also, a batting tee may be used for children who cannot hit a tossed ball.

### Five Hundred

*Formation.* Groups of children with open space for the children to scatter facing the batter.

```
              x x x x
   x       x x x x x
              x x x x
```

*Equipment.* One bat and two softballs.

*Number of Players.* Six to ten in each group.

*Game.* The batter, using "fungo" hits, sends the ball into the field toward the remainder of the players. The fielder closest to the ball fields the ball. If the ball is caught on the fly, the fielder gets one hundred points. If the ball is caught after one bounce, the fielder receives seventy-five points. If the ball is caught after two bounces, the fielder receives fifty points. If the ball is caught after three bounces, or before it stops rolling the fielder receives twenty-five points. The first player to receive five hundred points becomes the next batter and all players start again at zero.

*Teaching Suggestions.* A batting tee may be used for children who cannot hit a tossed ball. Also, for children who field the ball well, points may be subtracted from their score for making an error.

*Pepper*

*Formation.* Children standing in a line about forty-five to fifty feet from the batter.

```
                          X
                          X
              X
                          X
                          X
```

*Equipment.* One bat and two softballs.

*Number of Players.* Six to ten in each group.

*Game.* Using an easy overhand throw, one player in the line throws the ball to the batter. The batter, using a modified swing with no wrist snap, hits the ball at a moderate speed toward the line of fielders. The fielder in front of the ball fields the ball and throws it to the batter. This process should be repeated as quickly as possible to keep the batter busy.

If a fielder makes an error, he moves to the end of the line. If the batter hits the ball over the fielder's heads or swings and misses once, he takes his place at the end of the line and the fielder at the top of the line becomes the new batter.

*Teaching Suggestions.* When the children are batting, caution them to use a correct swing but no wrist snap. Also, the players in the fielding line should use a good ready position to be ready to field the ball.

*Work-up*

*Formation.* Regular softball positions in the field with three or four batters.

*Equipment.* One softball, a bat, three bases, and a home plate.

*Number of Players.* Twelve to fourteen players.

*Game.* The game is played and started with regular softball rules. If a fielder should catch a fly ball, he becomes the batter. When the batter makes an out which is not a caught fly ball, he becomes the right fielder and all the fielders move up one position. The rotation is from right to center field, center field to left field, left field to shortstop, shortstop to third base, from third to second and to first base, first base to pitcher, and pitcher to catcher. The catcher becomes the last batter. The players may also rotate to the umpire positions.

*Teaching Suggestions.* When the hitting and pitching skills are not consistent, a batting tee may be used to speed up the game.

The batters waiting their turn to bat should remain in the dugout in a safe area. To prevent throwing the bat, the batter may be required either to carry the bat toward first base with him, or to place one end of the bat on the ground before releasing the bat.

### SHOOTING SKILLS

*Two-Hand Underhand Shot.* Stand with the feet slightly spread. Hold the ball with the fingers, both hands slightly under the ball. Bend the knees slightly as the ball. Bend the knees slightly as the ball swings down between the knees (Fig. 9-29). Swing the ball forward and upward and at the same time shift the body weight up on balls of feet. Release the ball at about eye level. Follow through toward the basket.

Figure 9-29

*Two-Hand Chest Shot.* Stand with one foot slightly in front of the other. Hold the ball with the fingers spread, in front of the chest, and elbows close to side. Bend the knees slightly. Push the ball forward and upward and then extend the knees (Fig. 9-30). Release the ball above eye level with a wrist snap. Follow through toward the basket.

Figure 9-30                    Figure 9-31

*One-Hand Push Shot.* Put the right foot ahead of the left. Hold the ball in the left hand against the right hand with the fingers. Shift the weight forward as the ball is pushed upward. Release the ball above eye level with a snap of the wrist and fingers. Follow through toward the basket (Fig. 9-31).

### Shooting Skill Progression

The following skills are listed progressively:
  1. Shoot the ball through a hoop hung from a basket.

2. Shoot the ball into a barrel standing on the floor.

3. Shoot the ball into a barrel which is supported by a table.

4. Shoot the ball at the rim of the standard basket.

5. Shoot the ball into the basket while standing within five feet of the basket.

6. Shoot the ball into the basket while standing in the free-throw circle (Fig. 9-32).

Figure 9-32                    Figure 9-33

7. Shoot the ball into the basket while standing behind the free-throw line.

8. Shoot the ball while running (lay-up).

9. Shoot the ball while jumping (Fig. 9-33).

10. Shoot the ball with back to the basket (hook shot).

*Teaching Suggestion.* For small childen use a lighter ball. A partially deflated ball may help some children to find success.

## Basketball Skill Games

### *Basketball Keep-Away*

*Formation.* Children in a single circle facing the center of the circle.

*Equipment.* One basketball for each circle.

*Number of Players.* Six to eight in each group.

*Game.* One player goes to the center of the circle. The circle players pass the ball across the circle. The center player attempts to touch the ball. If he is successful he takes the position of the player who threw the ball.

*Teaching Suggestion.* For practice or variation change the type of pass used by the group.

### *Rotten Egg Basketball*

*Formation.* Children in a line with a basket at the end of the line.

*Equipment.* One basketball and a box or wastebasket.

*Number of Players.* Three to six.

*Game.* The children are in a line. A box or basket is placed at the end of the line. The ball is placed on the floor at the other end of the line approximately six feet from the last player. The last player runs to get the ball. He passes the ball to the next person in the line. Each player in turn passes the ball to the next player. The last player throws the ball (rotten egg) into the basket. Players rotate positions and the ball is placed on the floor to begin the relay again.

*Teaching Suggestions.* The distance between players may be increased as the passing skill improves. Also, the height of the box may be changed upward as the skill of the players improves. The final step would be to use a standard basket.

### *School*

*Formation.* Children stand in a column behind first grade.

*Equipment.* One basketball for each group.

*Number of Players.* Three to six in each group.

*Game.* Players number off and shoot in that order through the game. Player No. 1 shoots from the first-grade circle. If he is successful in making a field goal, he continues and shoots from the second-grade circle. When he misses, he stays at that grade level and waits for his next turn. The shooter retrieves his own ball after each shot. Players continue to shoot at the basket in the order in which they are numbered, regardless of the grade they are in. When his second turn comes, he shoots from the grade level where he missed his last shot.

The player wins who is first successful in making a basket from each grade level. He then retrieves the ball while the other players complete the game.

*Teaching Suggestions.* Specify the kind of shot to be used if the children are on equal level of ability. A barrel may be used for beginners.

### Follow the Leader

*Formation.* Children in a column formation behind the free-throw line.

*Equipment.* One basketball for each group.

*Number of Players.* Three to six.

*Game.* Player No. 1 shoots from any line on the floor he chooses. If Player No. 1 does not make a basket, Player No. 2 may choose any line on the floor from which to make his shot. If Player No. 1 makes the basket, Player No. 2 must shoot from the same spot on the floor. After completing his turn, each player returns to the end of the column behind the free-throw line.

*Teaching Suggestions.* A barrel may be used for beginners. As the skill improves, different types of shooting may be required.

### Ten Baskets

*Formation.* Children in a column formation behind the free-throw line.

*Equipment.* One basketball for each group and a set of numbers for each group.

*Number of Players.* Two to six.

*Game.* Player No. 1 shoots from anywhere in the foul lane. If he makes the basket he goes to the scoreboard and turns up the number one card. Each player in turn shoots once at the basket.

If a basket is made, he turns up the next number. After completing a turn, each player returns to the end of the column. Each player retrieves his own ball and passes it to the next player in the column. The first team to reach ten is the winning team.

*Teaching Suggestion.* For variation each team could try to improve the number of baskets made in a time limit.

## Lead-up Games to Basketball

### *Captain Ball*

*Formation.* Basketball court with five circles on each half of the court.

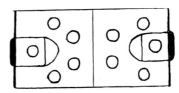

*Equipment.* One basketball.

*Number of Players.* Ten on each team.

*Game.* Five forwards on each team occupy the circles on their half of the court. The guards stand outside the circles on their opponents' half of the court. The game is started in the center of the floor with a jump ball by two opposing guards. The guards dribble and pass the ball to the center line, where they pass the ball to one of their forwards in a circle. The forwards try to pass the ball to the captain, who is in the circle closest to the basket. One point is given each time the ball is passed successfully to the captain. Each time a point is made, the players on both sides of the floor rotate one position.

Players may not step on the lines forming the circles or on the sidelines or center line. For a violation, the ball is awarded to the closest opponent. Personal contact is a foul for which the player fouled is given a free throw.

*Teaching Suggestions.* For players with good shooting ability, the game may be varied so the captain shoots upon receiving the ball. The points are scored the same as for regular basketball.

If considerable time elapses before a score is made, time may be called and the players rotate.

### Sideline Basketball

*Formation.* Players from each team line up along their respective sidelines.

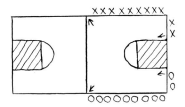

*Equipment.* One ball, one half of a basketball court, pinnies to designate team identity.

*Number of Players.* Sixteen to thirty-two players.

*Game.* Two players from each team move onto the court from the basket end of their sideline. Begin the game with a jump ball in the restraining circle. The team gaining possession of the ball becomes the offensive or shooting team. When the ball is intercepted by the opposing team, they must pass the ball to their sideline players before they can shoot for a basket. The team in possession of the ball may shoot successive shots until the other team gains possession of the ball.

After a goal is made, or after a time limit, the active players rotate to the sideline near the center line and the four sideline players nearest the basket become the active players. The sideline players may not step over the sideline. The active players should be encouraged to use the sideline players as teammates by passing the ball to them.

Regulation basketball rules may be applied.

*Teaching Suggestions.* This game provides an opportunity for inexperienced children to learn the rules. To provide for height differences, line the players up on the sideline with the tallest players on the same end of the line.

### Twenty-One

*Formation.* Players assume positions for a free throw, with one team in the offensive position.

*Equipment.* One basketball, one basket, and pinnies to designate team identity.

*Number of Players.* Two to five on each team.

*Game.* One player from the offensive team shoots from the free-throw line. He continues to shoot from the free-throw line until he misses or makes three consecutive baskets. Each free throw counts one point. If the shooter makes three baskets the ball is awarded to the opposing team out of bounds at the center line.

When the shooter misses and if his team gets possession of the ball, they may continue to shoot at the basket. If the defensive team gets possession of the ball they must dribble or pass the ball to a point at least twenty feet away from the basket to give the defense a chance to set up.

The play continues until someone on either team makes a field goal, which counts two points. The player making the field goal moves to the free-throw line and repeats the process used to start the game. The game continues until one team gets twenty-one points. If a team should end up with twenty-two points, their score becomes eleven and they must work their way up to twenty-one again.

*Teaching Suggestions.* Encourage the players to call three-second lane violations and other infractions of the rules. Stress passing and teamwork.

# Chapter 10

# SWIMMING

Swimming is accepted as being important for the normal child, and it is doubly important for the child with learning disabilities. The retarded child has been cheated in his ability to make judgments, to understand fears, to make choices, and to remember warnings and cautions. There seems to be a natural attraction between a child and the water; all children are drawn to water, with its movement and mysterious colors and shapes. Every child is captured by the water and is drawn to this fascinating hazard that can be his total undoing without performing skill and swimming ability on his part.

The general outline for the teaching of swimming to the non-swimmer is essentially the same for the retarded child and for the child with learning disabilities as it is for the normal child. Each learner must make a progressive advance along the skill chart in order to become a skilled swimmer. The retarded child usually will progress more slowly than will the normal child. The teacher must be prepared to spend a great amount of time on each skill, and because of the seemingly slow progress being made her patience will often be tested. Each class period will be a help to the child in the learning of his swimming skill. Even those lessons in which the child appears to have learned nothing and has made no progress will eventually help make him more skilled in the water.

## OBJECTIVES OF THE SWIMMING PROGRAM

The objectives of the special education swimming program may be listed as follows:

1. The first objective of any swimming program is to teach the child to swim. This is especially true of a swimming program for the child with learning problems, because safety in the water is of first concern.

2. Swimming may serve as a tool for a retarded child to be-

come a member of a group. This may be the only group experience in which he is truly a participating member.

3. Swimming offers a child the opportunity to experience success while experiencing fun.

4. Swimming, because it may be a new experience, may help to increase the attention span of a child. This may carry over into other activities and thus enrich his total learning experience.

5. Swimming may be the one activity in which the retarded child can share equally with the members of his family.

6. Swimming can be a great contributor to the physical fitness of the performer. The retarded child usually has not participated in games and exercise programs and consequently needs to improve his physical well-being.

7. Swimming may help the child to develop his ability to follow directions. This may affect his ability to follow directions in his schoolwork and in his activities at home.

The overall objective of the aquatic program should be to increase the potential of the child by enlarging the horizons for his total experiences. Swimming may be the key to increased success and his step-by-step progress out of the total darkness.

## PROGRAM ORGANIZATION

*Safety.* The organization for a swimming program for the mentally handicapped is like any other well-organized swimming program. It must be thoroughly understood that swimming is a dangerous activity and that a mistake in judgment on the part of the director or by the instructor may result in an accident for one of the students. *Safety* must be the first consideration with any swimming program.

*Pool.* Any available pool should be included in the planning. There are many nonscheduled hours in most pools. These hours are the least desirable ones for the public. They may come during the morning when children are in school and mothers are home with housework, or they may be at noon or at normal dinner hours. Pool owners can usually be encouraged to make the pool available for special education use during these hours, very often free of charge.

*Times.* Learning is better with frequent short periods of instruction than it is with infrequent long periods of instruction. It is better to have two groups swim twice a week for thirty minutes each than to have each group swim once a week for an hour. When the class periods come once a week, the nonpracticing time is too long; this results in too much time in which to forget and the teacher is always starting over.

*Instructors.* It is necessary to have one instructor for every trainable student and one instructor for every nonswimming educable student. An instructor can handle four or five swimming-educable students. These standards require a large number of instructors. The person in charge of the program should be well trained in aquatics—training by the Young Men's Christian Association, the Boy Scouts of America, or the American Red Cross is essential and readily available. The more practical knowledge and experience each instructor has, the better the instruction in the program will be. Persons who themselves are good swimmers can make excellent instructors when given assistance and guidance by the trained director. All communities have trained swimming people who are willing to volunteer their services if the need for their assistance were made known. Often volunteer service is as reliable as paid service and can give the program community contacts that will help in all areas of service in special education.

Another source of instructors lies with the parents of each child. Even if these persons are not trained swimming teachers, they can be taught to be instructor aides and can help in giving swimming instruction.

*Suits.* Parents can usually provide a swim suit for their own child, but a child should not be excluded from the program because of a parent's inability to provide a suit. Most swimming families have outgrown suits and will be eager to put them to a good use.

*Cautions.* All children in the swimming program should have a permission card signed by the family physician and by the parents. Special attention must be paid to the child who is subject to convulsive seizures. This child should not be excluded just because of the seizures, but he should have his physician's permission for swimming. Someone responsible for this particular child and someone experienced in handling the seizure should be at the pool edge at all times. The swimming instructor should not be expected to handle this problem.

Children should be encouraged to get thoroughly dry following the swimming period. Children may be subject to colds, and wet hair will compound this problem. If each child brings an extra towel, he can get dry enough to keep from getting chilled.

## METHODS OF INSTRUCTION

The American Red Cross suggests that emphasis should be placed upon breath control, the face-down float and recovery to standing position, and the face-up float and recovery to standing position. These three skills are basic to all swimming, and when a child can perform them successfully he is ready for more exciting and challenging swimming.

An instructor should work in the water with the child as long as the child is involved in learning the basic skills of swimming. This will give the child confidence in the ability of the instructor to help him. It is safe for the child and makes it possible for the instructor to share the water experiences with the child.

As soon as the child can perform the basic skills he should be placed in a group for instruction—the sooner a child can function in a group the sooner he will be able to live in a group and swimming can be a great help in preparing a child for successful group participation. It will also free an instructor to assist another beginning child and thus increase the number of participants that a limited number of instructors can teach.

Other methods of instruction are basic to all physical education instruction and are listed in Chapter 1.

### Swimming Skill Progression

The following list of skills is presented in an organization easy for the instructor to follow. The list is presented in a step-by-step procedure in which one skill builds upon the preceding one. The instructor should become acquainted with the list so that he is able to move smoothly from one skill to the next. At the end of each lesson he should check on the skill sheet the progress made by the child.

### Adjustment to the Water

These first nine skills are designed to help the child adjust to the water:

1. Hold the child in your arms and gently bounce with him in the water. Do not splash or duck him or allow him to splash on other children.

2. Go a little farther under the water each time and stay a little longer each time.

3. Let the water drop from your hand onto his shoulder, his hair, his chest, his chin, and his nose. Do not toss the water at him; just let it drop onto him (Fig. 10-1). Encourage him to do this to you.

Figure 10-1

4. Hold the child at the underarms and gently swing him from side to side and forward and backward.

5. Hold the child at the underarms and circle with him slowly; then circle with him fast. Keep his head up and let him feel the water flow past him.

6. Take hold of both of the child's hands, and pull him slowly forward (Fig. 10-2). His face is out of the water.

Figure 10-2

7. Take hold of both of the child's hands, and circle with him. Practice number 6 and number 7 several times. Explore the pool, talk to the child, and show him new places in the pool.

8. Repeat number 7 and have the child kick. Tell him to kick hard and make a big splash while you pull the child fast.

9. Have the child take hold of the edge of the pool. The instructor takes hold of the child's feet and helps the child kick from the hips and with a slight bend at the knees. There is no need to stress to the child the direction of the kick if the child is helped through the kicking process.

### Front Swimming Stroke—Crawl

Mastery of the next nineteen skills will enable the child to swim the crawl:

10. Stand in shallow water with the child. Take a deep breath, shut your lips, close your eyes, and put your face in the water. Come up and wipe the water from your eyes and smile. Have the child do this for you.

11. The instructor can use tricks to keep the child interested. Straws to blow through, table tennis balls and balloons to blow along the water (Fig. 10-3), and pennies, rocks, and diving rings on the bottom of the pool will all help to get him under the water and used to the feel of water in his hair and eyes.

Figure 10-3

12. Take hold of both of the child's hands. Have him put his face in the water (Fig. 10-4).

Figure 10-4

13. Take hold of both of the child's hands. The instructor pulls the child and the child puts his face in the water.

14. Ask the child to put his face in the water without the instructor holding his hands.

15. The instructor should move about three feet away from the child and encourage the child to put his face in the water and

walk to the instructor while his face is in the water.

16. The instructor should extend both of his arms and have the child grasp with both of his hands the left arm and wrist of the instructor. The instructor's right arm is under the child's body to give added support. Pull the child forward (Fig. 10-5).

Figure 10-5

17. Repeat number 16. Pull the child forward with his face in the water.

18. Repeat number 17 and have the child kick as he is pulled forward.

19. Stand a few feet from the edge of the pool in about three feet of water. Hold the child at the waist. The child extends his arms and puts his face in the water. The instructor pushes the child to the edge of the pool with enough force to get him to the edge but not enough to crash him into the edge (Fig. 10-6).

20. Repeat number 19 several times, increasing the distance from the edge of the pool each time.

21. Repeat number 20 and have the child kick as the instructor pushes him to the edge of the pool.

22. In shallow water the instructor should face the child and

Figure 10-6

take hold of both of his hands. The instructor moves the child's arms through the crawl pattern (Fig. 10-7).

Figure 10-7

23. Have the child move his arms in the crawl pattern without the instructor's aiding in the pattern.

24. Have the child put his face in the water and move his arms through the crawl pattern.

25. The instructor holds the child at his waist in about three feet of water and about five feet from the edge of the pool. The child puts his face in the water. The instructor pushes the child toward the edge of the pool and the child kicks and moves his arms through the crawl pattern.

26. Repeat number 25 several times, increasing the distance from the edge of the pool each time.

27. Teach the child to regain a standing position: From a front floating position bring both knees to the chest and pull down with both arms. Raise the head, force the feet to the bottom of the pool, and stand up. This should be practiced until the child can regain his standing position from a front float easily.

28. Have the child stand on the bottom of the pool, push off, and swim. Practice many times, increasing the distance to be covered each time.

### Back Swimming Position—Finning Backstroke

The ten skills that follow will enable the child to do the finning backstroke:

29. The instructor should stand behind the child and have the child lie on his back. The instructor should support the child at his shoulder blades or at his armpits (Fig. 10-8). A gentle nudge on the child's seat with the instructor's knee will get the child's hips in a floating position.

Figure 10-8

30. The instructor should pull the child across the pool. The child's head should be back and his arms at his sides.

31. Have the child take a breath of air and hold it. The instructor then removes one of his hands and returns it to position. Repeat with the other hand being removed and finally both hands being removed and replaced while the child is floating.

32. Repeat number 31 several times, increasing the amount of time the instructor's hands are removed from under the child's shoulders.

33. Repeat number 32 and have the child kick. Pull the child across the pool and have him kick and float by himself some of the distance.

34. Have the child hold onto the edge of the pool with his knees between his hands. Ask him to lie back on the water, keep his chin up, and kick his feet. The instructor should be ready to catch the child when the forward movement stops.

35. Repeat number 34 several times, increasing the distance to be covered. The instructor catches the child when the forward movement stops.

36. Teach the child to regain a standing position. Sweep both arms toward the feet, bend at the hips, forcefully extend the legs toward the bottom of the pool, and stand up. Practice many times until the child can regain a standing position easily.

37. Have the child do a back float; bring his hands up the sides of his body to the armpits and push them back down along the body. Keep the arms close to the body.

38. Have the child do a back float and kick and do the finning pattern with the arms.

### Combined Skills

These last nine of the progression are combinations of the skills already learned:

39. Have the child do a front swimming stroke and turn over to the back swimming position. The instructor should give aid if needed at the time of the turning over. Stress the child's doing a strong kick immediately upon turning over.

40. Have the child combine the crawl, finning, and turning

over. Sometimes start on the back, turn over, and finish with the crawl. The child should be able to turn from either position easily and continue swimming.

41. Have the child jump into waist-deep water. If necessary the instructor can catch the child the first few times.

42. Have the child jump into the water (Fig. 10-9), push off the pool bottom, swim and turn over, and swim to the other side of the pool.

Figure 10-9

43. Have the child jump into deeper water. Progress slowly. Orient the child to be in the water without the teacher also being in the water. Teach the child to respond to signals and to reach for a pole if he needs assistance. Do not allow the child to grab at the instructor when working in deep water.

44. Practice the crawl and turning over and finning combinations in deep water.

45. Have the child jump into deep water.

46. Have the child jump, level off, and swim in deep water.

This list is a step-by-step experience that is designed to help the instructor build skill upon skill to increase the swimming ability of the children in the program. The best way to drown-proof a person is to help him become the best swimmer that he can be. He must understand the dangers around the pool and he must understand and have respect for the pool organization.

The following Swimming Skill Chart can be used by the children to record their progress.

## SWIMMING SKILL CHART

| | Date | | | | | | | |
|---|---|---|---|---|---|---|---|---|
| Get into water. | | | | | | | | |
| Drop water on head. | | | | | | | | |
| Teacher pulls you. | | | | | | | | |
| Teacher pulls and you kick. | | | | | | | | |
| Hold to side and kick. | | | | | | | | |
| Put face in water. | | | | | | | | |
| Teacher pulls — You put face in water. | | | | | | | | |
| Teacher pulls — Face in water — You kick. | | | | | | | | |
| Walk to teacher — Face in water. | | | | | | | | |
| Front float. | | | | | | | | |
| Teacher pushes you to pool edge. | | | | | | | | |
| Teacher pushes and You kick. | | | | | | | | |
| Move arms for The crawl. | | | | | | | | |
| Teacher pushes — You move arms. | | | | | | | | |
| Swim Crawl. | | | | | | | | |
| Teacher holds you for back float. | | | | | | | | |
| Back float. | | | | | | | | |
| Back float and kick. | | | | | | | | |
| Back float and kick and move arms. | | | | | | | | |
| Turn from front to back — Keep floating. | | | | | | | | |
| Turn from back to front — Keep floating. | | | | | | | | |
| Jump into shallow water. | | | | | | | | |
| Jump into Deep water. | | | | | | | | |
| Jump and swim. | | | | | | | | |

## EXAMPLE OF INTEGRATION INTO THE CLASSROOM OF A PHYSICAL EDUCATION UNIT OF INSTRUCTION

The following is an example of using a physical education activity unit in the classroom. This integration will put an emphasis on the activity or gymnasium experience and will give a double exposure of the activity concepts for use by the students in their school environment.

The example selected is that of swimming. The actual swimming skills will be taught by the trained swimming specialist and the classroom concepts will be taught by the special education teacher in the classroom. Team teaching cooperation will be required in order for the unit to be clearly and profitably integrated.

This same approach of integration can be used with each of the other instructional units.

### OBJECTIVES OF THE SWIMMING PROGRAM

The objectives of a swimming program are as follows:
1. For the child to be able to swim.
    a. To be able to put his face into the water.
    b. To be able to open his eyes under water.
    c. To be able to change position in the water.
    d. To be able to swim comfortably in the prone position.
    e. To be able to swim comfortably in the back position.
2. For the child to develop an appreciation of the value and joy of participation in aquatic activities.
3. For the child to understand the safety factors involved in aquatic activities.

### CLASSROOM CONCEPTS FOR SWIMMING

The classroom concepts are the following:
1. A good swimmer is a safe swimmer.
2. A good swimmer is a good citizen.
3. A good swimmer knows how to float on his front and back.
4. A good swimmer knows how to kick.
5. A good swimmer knows how to turn over.
6. A good swimmer knows how to do the crawl stroke.
7. A good swimmer knows how to swim the elementary backstroke.

    8.  A good swimmer knows artificial respiration.

I.  *A Good Swimmer Is a Safe Swimmer.*
- A.  Experience Chart
    1. We get into our suits quickly.
    2. We walk to the shower.
    3. We walk to the pool.
    4. We sit on the bench and wait for the teachers.
    5. We walk to the edge of the pool and sit on the edge.
- B.  Spelling Words

    | | | | |
    |---|---|---|---|
    | 1. | safety | 7. | pool |
    | 2. | showers | 8. | sport |
    | 3. | walk | 9. | towel |
    | 4. | deck | 10. | rope |
    | 5. | tile | 11. | beach |
    | 6. | suit | 12. | lake |

- C.  Student Activities
    1. Discuss why children should learn to swim.
    2. Cut out catalog pictures of people in swim suits.
    3. Copy spelling words.
    4. Check on chart your own swimming skills—to be done when the child returns from the pool.
- D.  Teacher Activities
    1. Help with the discussion of why children should learn to swim.
    2. Explain the swimming program.
    3. Design the bulletin board.
    4. Write the spelling words.
    5. Prepare the swimming chart.
    6. Read a story about swimming.
- E.  Materials Needed
    1. Catalog.
    2. Scissors, paper, glue, colored paper.

II.  *A Good Swimmer Is a Good Citizen.*
- A.  Experience Chart
    1. We are quiet and polite on the bus.
    2. We are quite and polite in the dressing rooms.
    3. We are polite to the dressing-room helpers.
    4. We listen to our teachers.

5. We keep our hands to ourselves.
6. We are careful to splash only ourselves.

B. Spelling Words
   1. teacher
   2. teach
   3. fun
   4. alone
   5. friends
   6. class
   7. swim
   8. bus

C. Student Activities
   1. Discuss why we should listen to our teachers.
   2. Copy spelling words.
   3. Write a story about the swimming pool.
   4. Draw the pool and put a child in the picture.
   5. Check on the chart your own swimming skills.

D. Teacher Activities
   1. Discuss the rules of behavior at the pool.
   2. Write the spelling words.
   3. Read with the children their stories.
   4. Display their pictures.
   5. Read a story about swimming.

E. Materials Needed
   1. Paper for stories.
   2. Art paper and crayons.

III. *A Good Swimmer Knows How to Float.*

A. Experience Chart
   1. We can hold our breath.
   2. We can get our faces wet.
   3. We smile as we wipe the water away.
   4. We get our hair wet.
   5. We put water on the top of our own head.
   6. We let our feet come off the pool bottom.

B. Spelling Words
   1. face
   2. water
   3. feet
   4. nose
   5. mouth
   6. breath
   7. children
   8. hair
   9. float
   10. wade
   11. jellyfish

C.  Student Activities
1.  Discuss family outings involving water activities.
2.  Copy spelling words.
3.  Discuss how its feels to put your face in the water.
4.  Check off skills on the chart.

D.  Teacher Activities
1.  Display American Red Cross posters on safety—available from the local Red Cross office.
2.  Copy spelling words.
3.  Ask children to bring newspaper articles and magazine articles about swimming.
4.  Read a story about swimming.

E.  Materials Needed
1.  Posters.
2.  Paper.

IV.  *A Good Swimmer Knows How to Kick.*
A.  Experience Chart
1.  We float on our front.
2.  We let the water support us.
3.  We keep our legs straight when we kick.
4.  We hold our breath under water.

B.  Spelling Words

| | | | |
|---|---|---|---|
| 1. front | 7. underwater |
| 2. flutter | 8. practice |
| 3. inhale | 9. toes |
| 4. exhale | 10. knees |
| 5. cool | 11. kickboard |
| 6. warm | 12. chest |

C.  Student Activities
1.  Draw a swimming poster.
2.  Copy the spelling words.
3.  Write a story about learning to swim.
4.  Check off swimming skills.

D.  Teacher Activities
1.  Display posters.
2.  Write spelling words.
3.  Show old-fashioned swimming suits—available from costume houses.

    4. Ask children to save plastic bleach bottles, one-gallon size.

    5. Buy some tropical fish to watch swim.

  E. Materials Needed

    1. Art paper for posters.

    2. Scissors, crayons, glue.

    3. Swim suits.

V. *A Good Swimmer Knows How to Turn Over.*

  A. Experience Chart

    1. We know our fronts.

    2. We know our backs.

    3. We raise one arm over our heads and turn over toward it.

  B. Spelling Words

| | | | |
|---|---|---|---|
| 1. back | | 5. downward |
| 2. eyes | | 6. board |
| 3. arms | | 7. side |
| 4. upward | | 8. edge |

  C. Student Activities

    1. Discuss why the modern suits they wear at the pool are more safe to wear than the old-fashioned suits.

    2. Copy spelling words.

    3. Use spelling words in sentences about swimming activities.

    4. Check off swimming skills.

  D. Teacher Activities

    1. Write spelling words.

    2. Read a story about swimming.

    3. Go with the children to catch frogs and observe how they swim.

VI. *A Good Swimmer Knows How to Swim the Crawl Stroke.*

  A. Experience Chart

    1. We know how to kick.

    2. We know how to move our arms for the crawl stroke.

    3. We can kick and move our arms at the same time.

B.  Spelling Words
1.  stroke
2.  exercise
3.  aquatic
4.  reach
5.  catch
6.  pull
7.  breathe

C.  Student Activities
1.  Copy spelling words.
2.  Go to the pool and observe the swimmers from the underwater windows.
3.  Draw the underwater swimmers.
4.  Check off swimming skills.

D.  Teacher Activities
1.  Write the spelling words.
2.  Take the children to look through the underwater windows.
3.  Display the pictures of underwater swimmers.
4.  Read a story about skin diving.

E.  Materials Needed
1.  Art paper.
2.  Scissors.
3.  Glue.

VII.  *A Good Swimmer Knows the Elementary Backstroke.*

A.  Experience Chart
1.  We can float on our back.
2.  We can open our eyes.
3.  We can breathe.

B.  Spelling Words
1.  family
2.  group
3.  deep
4.  shallow
5.  Red Cross

C.  Student Activities
1.  Copy spelling words.
2.  Write an invitation to the Red Cross instructor trainer or water safety instructor to come next week and talk about artificial respiration.
3.  Check off swimming skills.

D. Teacher Activities
  1. Write spelling words.
  2. Accompany the children to the Red Cross office to deliver the invitation. Call ahead and make arrangements.
  3. Remind the children about the plastic bottles.

E. Materials Needed
  1. Paper for the invitation.

VIII. *A Good Swimmer Knows Artificial Respiration.*
  A. Experience Chart
    1. We are safe swimmers.
    2. We are good swimmers.
    3. We know something about beginning swimming.
    4. We need to know about artificial respiration.

  B. Spelling Words
    1. mouth
    2. nose
    3. blow
    4. stomach
    5. chin
    6. lungs
    7. artificial
    8. safety
    9. respiration
    10. accident

  C. Student Activities
    1. Copy spelling words.
    2. Listen carefully to the Red Cross instructor.

  D. Teacher Activities
    1. Write spelling words.
    2. Collect plastic bottles.

IX. *A Good Swimmer Knows Artificial Respiration.*
  A. Experience Chart: Use the experiences listed on previous lesson.
  B. Student Activities: Make artificial respiration model with plastic bottle. (See Fig. 10-10.)
  C. Teacher Activities
    1. Cut off handle from an empty one-gallon bleach bottle one inch from top of handle.
    2. Turn bottle upside down and handle side down.
    3. Use felt-tip pens and draw face.

4. Cut out a hole for mouth.
5. Attach a plastic sack to the handle of the bottle.
6. Tape up the hole at the top of the bottle.
7. Tape a book to the bag so that when the bag fills with air the weight of the book presses down upon the bag and forces the air out.

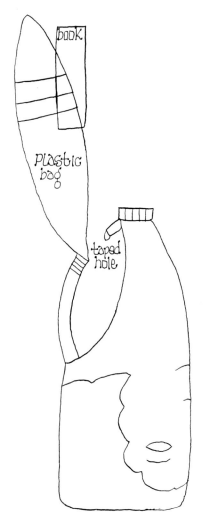

Figure 10-10. Artificial respiration model.

D. Materials Needed
   1. Plastic bottle for each child.
   2. Plastic sack for each child.
   3. Tape.
   4. Felt-tip pens.

# Chapter 11

# TRACK AND FIELD

T RACK AND FIELD events provide good self-testing activities in which each child can challenge himself at his own level of ability. The conditioning inherent in the performance of these activities makes them valuable components of any program. Running, jumping, and throwing are basic skills used in most sports and games, and therefore the ability to perform them well will enhance the enjoyment of other activities.

Several opportunities are available for handicapped children to participate in organized competition sponsored by service organizations. Many prominent citizens in the community are willing to contribute their means and time to foster opportunities for these children.

Track and field activities are easily adapted to provide for the differences in ability. Even children confined to wheelchairs can participate in many of the events. The nature of the activities provides natural incentive to participate. Everyone enjoys the thrill of running against the clock, the challenge of how far he can jump, or seeing how many feet he can throw a ball.

### Teaching Suggestions

The following are suggestions for the teacher of track and field activities:

1. Practice the events in a setting which is similar to the competitive situation.

2. Use immediate goals to challenge the children. Mentally retarded children need a mark or a flag as a target to help them realize their jumping ability.

3. When competition will be started with a starting gun, practice with the gun to acquaint the children with its meaning and its sound.

4. The use of immediate rewards, such as a ribbon or badge

with their achievement on it, will help the mentally retarded children to understand their accomplishments.

5. The children should warm up prior to participation in the event. Stretching exercises and light jogging are good. Reaching in all directions while sitting in the hurdle position will help develop the flexibility to perform this event.

6. Teach one event at a time and practice it until it becomes familar to the children. It should be reviewed when other events are being taught.

7. When more than one event is taking place, a leader for each event is needed.

8. When the children will be participating in competition, use the same type of equipment which will be used in the meet.

### 50-Yard Dash

See Chapter 2 for an additional analysis of the running skill.

*Crouch Start.* The following instructions are to be given:

1. "Take your marks." Place the foot of the front leg two hand-spans behind the starting line. Place the knee of the back leg even with the toes of the front foot, the thumb and forefinger parallel to the line with the fingers together, and focus the eyes down the track (Fig. 11-1).

Figure 11-1                    Figure 11-2

2. "Get set." Shift the weight up and forward to a position in which the weight is balanced on the hands and front foot, with some weight on the back foot, and the hips level with the shoulders (Fig. 11-2).

3. "Go!" Push off with the rear foot and vigorously extend the front leg. Step just in front of the line with the rear foot and reach forward with the opposite arm.

*Running the Dash.* For the first three or four steps, use the arms vigorously by reaching forward and backward in opposition. Use short, driving steps with high knee action and lean forward. Gradually rise to a slight leaning position and increase the size of each step until the standard running pace is reached.

While running the dash, lean slightly forward and relax as much as possible. Reach forward and backward with the arms (Fig. 11-3). The arms should be slightly bent and the hands should reach forward until they are about shoulder high and backward to the hip. Run on the balls of the feet with the toes pointed forward.

When finishing the race, run past the finish line at top speed and gradually slow to a jog and then a walk.

*Measurement.* The race may be against a stopwatch or against other children. It is easier to obtain the best performance when the children run against each other. Use a finish tape which will help the children to reach the end of the distance.

*Rules.* Everyone must be stationary before the starting signal. Everyone must run in his own lane.

*Variations.* The distance may be changed to meet the ability of the children. A 30-yard dash is good for younger children. A standing start may be used when it is difficult for the children to maintain their balance from a crouch start.

### 300-Yard Walk-Run

*Standing Start.* A forward-stride position should be assumed just behind the starting line. The knees, ankles, and hips should be slightly bent and the body should lean slightly forward in anticipation of the starting signal. With the signal to "get set," assume a position ready to push forward (Fig. 11-4). On the signal "go," push forward and move the arms in opposition and get into the normal running stride as soon as possible.

Figure 11-3                    Figure 11-4

*Running the Race.* Run at a pace which you can maintain over the required distance and still accomplish the distance in the shortest time possible. If the pace cannot be maintained, slow to a jogging or walking pace until the recovery is great enough to run again. Remember, the faster you can run, the better the time will be.

### 220-Yard Pursuit Relay

*Preparation.* Space four runners on each team fifty-five yards apart. The first runner assumes either a crouch-start position or a standing-start position, with the baton held by the lower half in the left hand. The other three runners assume a standing-start position facing the finish line.

*Running the Relay.* On the starting signal, Runner No. 1 races toward Runner No. 2. Runner No. 2 watches Runner No. 1

by looking over his shoulder. As Runner No. 1 approaches, Runner No. 2 extends the right arm back with the palm turned up, the fingers together, and the thumb out. When No. 1 gets about three yards away, No. 2 begins to run forward. No. 1 should place the baton into the hand of No. 2 firmly and both performers should watch the baton and hand during the exchange. (Note: More advanced runners may make the exchange using a blind pass with the second runner looking forward, as in (Fig. 11-5.) After receiving the baton, Runner No. 2 should transfer the baton to his left hand to carry it toward Runner No. 3. The same type of exchange is used by No. 2 and No. 3. No. 4 runs with the baton across the finish line.

Figure 11-5

*Rules.* Each runner must stay in his lane running and following the baton exchange until all runners have completed the exchange. The exchange of the baton must be done within twenty-two yards. If the baton should be dropped, the runner who last had possession must pick it up.

## 200-Yard Shuttle Relay

*Preparation.* Two runners for each team should be placed at each end of the 50-yard area. The first runner assumes either a crouch-start position or a standing-start position with the baton held vertically by the lower half in the right hand. The other three runners assume a standing-start position facing the approaching runner.

*Running the Relay.* On the starting signal, the first runner races toward the second runner. Runner No. 2 waits with the palm of the right hand facing Runner No. 1, with the fingers together and the thumb out. The first runner places the baton firmly in the hand of Runner No. 2 (Fig. 11-6). The second runner may begin running after receiving the baton from the first runner, but not before. The same procedure is used by the second and third runners. Runner No. 4 races across the finish line, which is the original starting line.

Figure 11-6

*Rules.* Each runner must stay in his lane. The receiver must stay behind the restraining line until the baton is received. If the baton should be dropped, the runner who last had possession must pick it up.

## 50-Yard Hurdle Race

*Preparation.* Four hurdles, $2\frac{1}{2}$ feet high, are needed for each lane. Place the hurdles 26 feet and $3\frac{1}{2}$ inches apart, with the first hurdle 39 feet and $4\frac{1}{2}$ inches from the starting line. The hurdles should be placed so they will tip forward if they should be hit by the performer.

*Running the Race.* The race is run like a 50-yard dash with the addition of the hurdles. The technique used to clear the hurdle should be similar to the normal running stride, not a jump. The lead leg is lifted toward the chest to extend the step over the hurdle (Fig. 11-7). The foot should land on the ground close to the hurdle to continue the running technique as quickly as possible. The trailing leg passes over the hurdle with the knee out to the side of the trunk and the toe turned out to avoid hitting the hurdle (Fig. 11-8). The body should lean into the reaching

Figure 11-7                    Figure 11-8

stride and the arms should reach in opposition. The trailing leg should snap down to regain the running position as soon as possible (Fig. 11-9). (Note: In teaching the hurdle technique, a rope held loosely can be held as low as necessary for the children to step over the rope. Gradually raise the rope and continue to work on the correct position of the front and trailing leg.)

*Rules.* Each runner must go over the hurdle with both legs.

Knocking down a hurdle is not a violation as long as the runner goes over it.

Each runner must stay in his own lane, and the other rules for running dashes should also be applied.

Figure 11-9

## Standing Long Jump

*Preparation.* A nonslip takeoff surface is needed. The landing surface should be turf or a mat with some give to absorb the force of the landing.

*Jumping Technique.* Stand with the toes behind the starting line. Assume a position with the weight on the balls of the feet, the arms bent and forward, and the knees and trunk bent in a sitting position (Fig. 11-10). Rock the weight back onto the heels and swing the arms backward (Fig. 11-11); then rock forward again as the arms swing forward into the jumping position. Extend the legs and trunk as the feet push upward and forward (Fig. 11-12). The arms should swing upward at a 45-degree angle with the head and chest lifted upward also. Lift the knees and reach forward with the legs to land on both feet (Fig. 11-13). Lean forward to prevent falling backward.

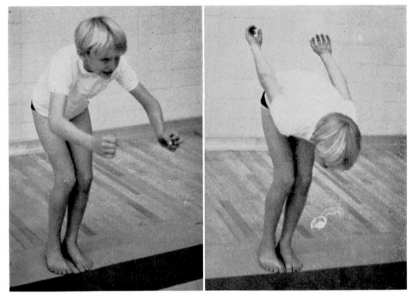

Figure 11-10                    Figure 11-11

Figure 11-12                    Figure 11-13

*Measurement.* The measurement is taken from the front edge of the takeoff board to the closest point of contact made by the performer.

*Rules.* The feet must be behind the takeoff board, both feet must be used, and no preparatory jump may be used.

## Running Long Jump

*Preparation.* A nonslip takeoff board and a landing pit with sand or sawdust in it is needed. The takeoff board should be preceeded by an approach area approximately 150 feet long.

*Jumping Technique.* Start on the takeoff board and run back the desired distance for the approach. Mark the point at which the foot to be used for jumping reached the desired approach distance. The takeoff should be long enough to reach approximately 80 percent of maximum speed and not tire the performer. The takeoff foot should hit the board with the knee and ankle bent, ready to extend (Fig. 11-14). As the push is made by the takeoff foot, the arms and head lift up at a 45-degree angle. The aim of the performer is to jump upward and let the forward speed carry the body forward as far as possible.

While in the air keep the head and chest up and reach forward with the legs into a sitting position. As the landing is made on both feet, swing the arms backward to thrust the body forward (Fig. 11-15).

Figure 11-14        Figure 11-15

*Rules.* The measurement is the same as that used for the standing long jump. The takeoff must be from one foot, and the foot must not be over the board.

## High Jump

*Preparation.* A pair of jump standards and a crossbar, and a soft landing pit are needed.

*Jumping Technique.* The jumper should start at least four or five strides from the crossbar. The approach should be from a 45-degree angle. The takeoff should be an arm's distance from the bar. The method of jumping may vary according to the jumper; the easiest method is the scissor jump. At the takeoff point, the push-off comes from the foot away from the bar. The leg closest to the bar is kicked up and over the bar while the arms swing upward to help life the body up (Fig. 11-16). The legs should be straight after the push-off. The performer passes over the bar in a sitting position and lands on one foot at a time.

Figure 11-16

A more advanced method of jumping is the straddle roll. The takeoff is on the foot closest to the bar. The outside leg kicks up and the arms swing upward (Fig. 11-17). After reaching the peak of the jump, roll over the bar and face it by turning the head and reaching wit the outside arm. Land facing the direction of the approach area on both feet and one arm, or on the shoulder and back if a sponge pit is used.

Figure 11-17

*Rules.* The measurement is from the upper edge of the crossbar to the ground. Each jumper is given three chances to clear each height. A third miss at any one height disqualifies the performer. A miss consists of knocking the bar off the standards.

### Softball Throw

*Preparation.* An approach area with a scratch line should be marked off at the edge of the throwing area. Markers should be available to mark the throw for each performer.

*Throwing Procedure.* See Chapter 9 for an analysis of the throwing technique. An overhand throw should be used by the contestant. When throwing for distance the release should be at a

45-degree angle (Fig. 11-18). Three trials are given the performer to achieve his greatest distance.

*Rules.* The performer may not step on or over the throwing line, and an overhand throw must be used.

*Measurement.* Measurement is the distance from the throwing line to the place where the ball first touched the ground. Only the best throw need be measured.

Figure 11-18                    Figure 11-19

## Soccer Throw

*Preparation.* Same as for the softball throw.

*Performance.* A soccer throw should be a sidearm throw. Start with the side to the throwing area. Hold the ball on the fingers and tucked against the forearm. With the weight on the back foot, swing the throwing arm backward and point the free arm toward the field. Two or three warm-up swings may be used to get momentum for the final release. On the last swing, the weight is transferred forward to rotate the hips and trunk, which in turn helps swing the arm forward and upward at a 45-degree angle (Fig. 11-19). Following the throw comes a reversal, in which the recovery of the body momentum by the back foot prevents falling over the line. The soccer throw is a good lead-up to the discus throw.

*Rules.* The performer may not step on or over the throwing line. Three trials are given the perfomer to achieve his greatest distance. Measurement is the distance from the throwing line to the place where the ball first touched the ground. Only the best throw need be measured.

# BIBLIOGRAPHY

American Association for Health, Physical Education, and Recreation: *Physical Activities for the Mentally Retarded*. Washington, D.C., AAHPER, 1968.

Anderson, Marian, Elliot, Margaret E., and LaBerge, Jeanne: *Play with a Purpose*. New York, Harper and Row, 1966.

Andrews, Gladys, Sanborn, Jeannette, and Schneider, Elsa: *Physical Education for Today's Boys and Girls*. Boston, Allyn and Bacon, 1960.

Barney, Vernon S., Hirst, Cyntha C., and Jensen, Clayne R.: *Conditioning Exercises*. St. Louis, C.V. Mosby, 1965.

Blake, William O., and Volp, Anne M.: *Lead-Up Games to Team Sports*. Englewood Cliffs, New Jersey, Prentice-Hall, 1964.

Boorman, Joyce: *Creative Dance in the First Three Grades*. New York, David McKay, 1969.

Braley, William T., Konicki, Geraldine, and Leedy, Catherine: *Daily Sensorimotor Training Activities*. Freeport, New York, Educational Activities Inc., 1968.

Bucher, Charles A., and Reade, Evelyn M.: *Physical Education and Health in the Elementary School*. New York, Macmillan, 1964.

Carlson, Bernice W., and Ginglend, David R.: *Play Activities for the Retarded Child*. New York, Abington Press, 1961.

Corder, W. Owens: Effects of physical education on the intellectual, physical, and social development of educable mentally retarded boys. *Exceptional Children, 32*:357-361, 1966.

Cratty, Bryant J.: *Motor Activity and the Education of Retardates*. Philadelphia, Lea and Febiger, 1969.

Drehamn, Garland, Jr.: *Head Over Heels*. New York, Harper and Row, 1967.

Fait, Hollis F.: *Special Physical Education: Adapted, Corrective, Developmental*. Philadelphia, W.B. Saunders, 1966.

Franklin, C.C., and Freeburg, William H.: *Diversified Games and Activities of Low Organization for Mentally Retarded Children*. Carbondale, Southern Illinois University.

Godfrey, Barbara B., and Kephart, Newell C.: *Movement Patterns and Motor Education*. New York, Appleton-Century-Crofts, 1969.

Hackett, Layne C., and Jenson, Robert G.: *A Guide to Movement Exploration*. Palo Alto, California, Peek Publications, 1966.

Hildreth, Gertrude: *Readiness for School Beginners*. New York, World Book Company, 1950.

Hughes, Eric: *Gymnastics for Girls*. New York, Ronald Press, 1963.

Humphrey, James H.: *Child Learning*. Dubuque, Iowa, Wm. C. Brown, 1965.

Jacobsen, Phyllis, and Valentine, Ann: *Fundamental Skills in Physical Education*. Provo, Utah, Brigham Young University, 1970.

Johnson, G. Orville: *Education for the Slow Learner*. Englewood Cliffs, New Jersey, Prentice-Hall, 1963.

Johnson, Warren R.: Critical periods, body image and movement competency in childhood. In *Report of a Symposium on Integrated Development*. N. Pub., N.P., 1964.

Joint Committee of the Council for Exceptional Children and American Association for Health, Physical Education, and Recreation! *Recreation and Physical Activity for the Mentally Retarded*. Washington, D.C., AAHPER, 1966.

Kephart, Newell C.: *The Slow Learner in the Classroom*. Columbus, Ohio, Charles E. Merrill, 1960.

Kirchner, Glenn, Cunningham, Jean, and Warrell, Eileen: *Introduction to Movement Education*. Dubuque, Iowa, Wm. C. Brown, 1970.

Kraus, Richard: *Play Activities for Boys and Girls*. New York, McGraw-Hill, 1957.

LaSalle, Dorothy: *Guidance of Children Through Physical Education*. New York, Ronald Press, 1957.

Monroe, Marion, Rogers, Bernice: *Foundations for Reading*. Chicago, Scott Foresman, 1964.

Nagel, Charles, and Moore, Fredericka: *Skill Development Through Games and Rhythmic Activities*. Palo Alto, California, National Press Books, 1966.

O'Quinn, Garland, Jr.: *Gymnastics for Elementary School Children*. Dubuque, Iowa, Wm. C. Brown, 1967.

Otto, Wayne, and McMenemy, Richard A.: *Corrective and Remedial Teaching*. Boston, Houghton Mifflin, 1966.

Perry, Natalie: *Teaching the Mentally Retarded Child*. New York, Columbia University, 1960.

Peter, Laurence J.: *Prescriptive Teaching*. New York, McGraw-Hill, 1965.

Radler, D.H., and Kephart, Newell C.: *Success Through Play*. New York, Harper and Row, 1960.

Rarick, G. Lawrence: How the Retarded Child Learns Through Physical Activity. Unpublished paper, University of Wisconsin.

Robins, Ferris and Janet: *Educational Rhythmics*. New York, Association Press, 1968.

Robinson, Helen M.: *Why Pupils Fail in Reading*. Chicago, University of Chicago, 1946.

Russell, David H., and Karp, Etta E.: *Reading Aids*. New York, Columbia University, 1956.

Salt, E. Benton, Salt, Grace I., and Stevens, B.K.: *Teaching Physical Education in the Elementary School.* New York, Ronald Press, 1960.

Schurr, Evelyn L.: *Movement Experiences for Children: Curriculum and Methods for Elementary School Physical Education.* New York, Appleton-Century-Crofts, 1967.

Stein, Julian: Motor function and physical fitness of the mentally retarded: A critical review. *Rehabilitation Literature,* Aug. 1963.

Taylor, Z. Ann, and Sherrill, Claudine: *A Health-Centered Core Curriculum for Educationally Handicapped Children.* Palo Alto, California, Peek Publications, 1969.

Troester, Carl A., Jr.: *Programing for the Mentally Retarded.* Washington, D.C., AAHPER, 1968.

Troester, Carl A., Jr.: *Special Fitness Test Manual for the Mentally Retarded.* Washington, D.C., AAHPER, 1968.

Wheeler, Ruth H., and Hooley, Agnes M.: *Physical Education for the Handicapped.* Philadelphia, Lea and Febiger, 1969.

# INDEX